MznLnx

Missing Links Exam Preps

Exam Prep for

Macroeconomics

Blanchard, 4th Edition

The MznLnx Exam Prep is your link from the texbook and lecture to your exams.
The MznLnx Exam Preps are unauthorized and comprehensive reviews of your textbooks.

All material provided by MznLnx and Rico Publications (c) 2010
Textbook publishers and textbook authors do not particpate in or contribute to these reviews.

MznLnx

Rico Publications

Exam Prep for Macroeconomics
4th Edition
Blanchard

Publisher: Raymond Houge
Assistant Editor: Michael Rouger
Text and Cover Designer: Lisa Buckner
Marketing Manager: Sara Swagger
Project Manager, Editorial Production: Jerry Emerson
Art Director: Vernon Lowerui

Product Manager: Dave Mason
Editorial Assitant: Rachel Guzmanji
Pedagogy: Debra Long
Cover Image: Jim Reed/Getty Images
Text and Cover Printer: City Printing, Inc.
Compositor: Media Mix, Inc.

(c) 2010 Rico Publications
ALL RIGHTS RESERVED. No part of this work covered by the copyright may be reproduced or used in any form or by an means--graphic, electronic, or mechanical, including photocopying, recording, taping, Web distribution, information storage, and retrieval systems, or in any other manner--without the written permission of the publisher.

Printed in the United States
ISBN:

For more information about our products, contact us at:
Dave.Mason@RicoPublications.com

For permission to use material from this text or product, submit a request online to:
Dave.Mason@RicoPublications.com

Contents

CHAPTER 1
A Tour of the World — 1

CHAPTER 2
A Tour of the Book — 6

CHAPTER 3
The Goods Market — 14

CHAPTER 4
Financial Markets — 21

CHAPTER 5
Goods and Financial Markets: The IS-LM Model — 29

CHAPTER 6
The Labor Market — 34

CHAPTER 7
Putting All Markets Together: The AS-AD Model — 39

CHAPTER 8
The Natural Rate of Unemployment and the Phillips Curve — 43

CHAPTER 9
Inflation, Activity, and Nominal Money Growth — 46

CHAPTER 10
The Facts of Growth — 49

CHAPTER 11
Saving, Capital Accumulation, and Output — 52

CHAPTER 12
Technological Progress and Growth — 55

CHAPTER 13
Technological Progress, Wages, and Unemployment — 60

CHAPTER 14
Expectations: The Basic Tools — 64

CHAPTER 15
Financial Markets and Expectations — 68

CHAPTER 16
Expectations, Consumption, and Investment — 74

CHAPTER 17
Expectations, Output, and Policy — 79

CHAPTER 18
Openness in Goods and Financial Markets — 81

CHAPTER 19
The Goods Market in an Open Economy — 87

CHAPTER 20
Output, the Interest Rate, and the Exchange Rate — 91

Contents (Cont.)

CHAPTER 21
Exchange Rate Regimes — 97

CHAPTER 22
Depressions and Slumps — 104

CHAPTER 23
High Inflation — 109

CHAPTER 24
Should Policy Makers Be Restrained? — 114

CHAPTER 25
Monetary Policy: A Summing Up — 119

CHAPTER 26
Fiscal Policy: A Summing Up — 128

CHAPTER 27
Epilogue: The Story of Macroeconomics — 133

ANSWER KEY — 141

TO THE STUDENT

COMPREHENSIVE

The *MznLnx* Exam Prep series is designed to help you pass your exams. Editors at MznLnx review your textbooks and then prepare these practice exams to help you master the textbook material. Unlike study guides, workbooks, and practice tests provided by the texbook publisher and textbook authors, *MznLnx* gives you **all** of the material in each chapter in exam form, not just samples, so you can be sure to nail your exam.

MECHANICAL

The MznLnx Exam Prep series creates exams that will help you learn the subject matter as well as test you on your understanding. Each question is designed to help you master the concept. Just working through the exams, you gain an understanding of the subject--its a simple mechanical process that produces success.

INTEGRATED STUDY GUIDE AND REVIEW

MznLnx is not just a set of exams designed to test you, its also a comprehensive review of the subject content. Each exam question is also a review of the concept, making sure that you will get the answer correct without having to go to other sources of material. You learn as you go! Its the easiest way to pass an exam.

HUMOR

Studying can be tedious and dry. MznLnx's instructional design includes moderate humor within the exam questions on occassion, to break the tedium and revitalize the brain

Chapter 1. A Tour of the World

1. The _____ was a worldwide economic downturn starting in most places in 1929 and ending at different times in the 1930s or early 1940s for different countries. It was the largest and most important economic depression in the 20th century, and is used in the 21st century as an example of how far the world's economy can fall. The _____ originated in the United States; historians most often use as a starting date the stock market crash on October 29, 1929, known as Black Tuesday.
   - a. Wall Street Crash of 1929
   - b. British Empire Economic Conference
   - c. Jarrow March
   - d. Great Depression

2. In economics, _____ is a rise in the general level of prices of goods and services in an economy over a period of time. When the general price level rises, each unit of currency buys fewer goods and services; consequently, _____ is also a decline in the real value of money--a loss of purchasing power in the medium of exchange which is also the monetary unit of account in the economy. A chief measure of general price-level _____ is the general _____ rate, which is the percentage change in a general price index (normally the Consumer Price Index) over time.
   - a. Energy economics
   - b. Opportunity cost
   - c. Inflation
   - d. Economic

3. In economics, the _____ is a measure of inflation, the rate of increase of a price index (for example, a consumer price index.)It is the percentage rate of change in price level over time. The rate of decrease in the purchasing power of money is approximately equal.

   It's used to calculate the real interest rate, as well as real increases in wages, and official measurements of this rate act as input variables to COLA adjustments and Inflation derivatives prices.

   - a. Edgeworth paradox
   - b. Interest rate option
   - c. Equity value
   - d. Inflation rate

4. Unemployment occurs when a person is available to work and seeking work but currently without work. The prevalence of unemployment is usually measured using the _____, which is defined as the percentage of those in the labor force who are unemployed. The _____ is also used in economic studies and economic indexes such as the United States' Conference Board's Index of Leading Indicators as a measure of the state of the macroeconomics.
   - a. AD-IA Model
   - b. ACCRA Cost of Living Index
   - c. ACEA agreement
   - d. Unemployment rate

5. A _____, reserve bank, or monetary authority is the entity responsible for the monetary policy of a country or of a group of member states. It is a bank that can lend money to other banks in times of need. Its primary responsibility is to maintain the stability of the national currency and money supply, but more active duties include controlling subsidized-loan interest rates, and acting as a lender of last resort to the banking sector during times of financial crisis (private banks often being integral to the national financial system.)
   - a. 130-30 fund
   - b. Central bank
   - c. 100-year flood
   - d. 1921 recession

6. The _____ was an evolution of developed countries from an industrial/manufacturing-based wealth producing economy into a service sector asset based economy, brought about by globalization and currency manipulation by governments and their central banks. Some analysts claimed that this change in the economic structure of the United States had created a state of permanent steady growth, low unemployment, and immunity to boom and bust macroeconomic cycles. They believed that the change rendered obsolete many business practices.

a. 1921 recession
b. 100-year flood
c. New Economy
d. 130-30 fund

7. _____ in economics refers to metrics and measures of output from production processes, per unit of input. Labor _____, for example, is typically measured as a ratio of output per labor-hour, an input. _____ may be conceived of as a metrics of the technical or engineering efficiency of production.
   a. Fordism
   b. Production-possibility frontier
   c. Productivity
   d. Piece work

8. To _____ is to impose a financial charge or other levy upon a taxpayer by a state or the functional equivalent of a state.

   _____es are also imposed by many subnational entities. _____es consist of direct _____ or indirect _____, and may be paid in money or as its labour equivalent (often but not always unpaid.)

   a. 130-30 fund
   b. 1921 recession
   c. Tax
   d. 100-year flood

9. A _____ is a reduction in taxes. Economic stimulus via _____s, along with interest rate intervention and deficit spending, are one of the central tenets of Keynesian economics.

   The immediate effects of a _____ are, generally, a decrease in the real income of the government and an increase in the real income of those whose tax rate has been lowered.

   a. Tax cut
   b. Popiwek
   c. Direct taxes
   d. Withholding tax

10. A _____ occurs when an entity spends more money than it takes in. The opposite of a _____ is a budget surplus. Debt is essentially an accumulated flow of deficits.
    a. Budget deficit
    b. Lump-sum tax
    c. Public Financial Management
    d. Funding body

11. _____ , as defined by the _____ Association of America (Information technologyAA), is 'the study, design, development, implementation, support or management of computer-based information systems, particularly software applications and computer hardware.' _____ deals with the use of electronic computers and computer software to convert, store, protect, process, transmit, and securely retrieve information.

    Today, the term _____ has ballooned to encompass many aspects of computing and technology, and the term has become very recognizable. The _____ umbrella can be quite large, covering many fields.

    a. AD-IA Model
    b. ACCRA Cost of Living Index
    c. Information technology
    d. ACEA agreement

12. _____ is generally measured by standards such as real (i.e. inflation adjusted) income per person and poverty rate. Other measures such as access and quality of health care, income growth inequality and educational standards are also used. Examples are access to certain goods (such as number of refrigerators per 1000 people), or measures of health such as life expectancy.
    a. 100-year flood
    b. Remuneration
    c. 130-30 fund
    d. Standard of living

13. The _____ is an economic and political union of 27 member states, located primarily in Europe. It was established by the Treaty of Maastricht on 1 November 1993, upon the foundations of the pre-existing European Economic Community. With a population of almost 500 million, the _____ generates an estimated 30% share (US$18.4 trillion in 2008) of the nominal gross world product.
    a. ACEA agreement
    b. European Union
    c. European Court of Justice
    d. ACCRA Cost of Living Index

14. _____s is the social science that studies the production, distribution, and consumption of goods and services. The term _____s comes from the Ancient Greek oá¼°κονομῖα from oá¼¶κος (oikos, 'house') + vÏŒμος (nomos, 'custom' or 'law'), hence 'rules of the house(hold)'. Current _____ models developed out of the broader field of political economy in the late 19th century, owing to a desire to use an empirical approach more akin to the physical sciences.
    a. Inflation
    b. Opportunity cost
    c. Economic
    d. Energy economics

15. The _____ is a concept of economic activity developed in particular by Milton Friedman and Edmund Phelps in the 1960s, both recipients of the Nobel prize in economics. In both cases, the development of the concept is cited as a main motivation behind the prize. It represents the hypothetical unemployment rate consistent with aggregate production being at the 'long-run' level.
    a. Real Business Cycle Theory
    b. Robertson lag
    c. Romer Model
    d. Natural rate of unemployment

16. The _____ is the official currency of 16 of the 27 member states of the European Union (EU.) The states, known collectively as the Eurozone, are Austria, Belgium, Cyprus, Finland, France, Germany, Greece, Ireland, Italy, Luxembourg, Malta, the Netherlands, Portugal, Slovakia, Slovenia, and Spain. The currency is also used in a further five European countries, with and without formal agreements and is consequently used daily by some 327 million Europeans.
    a. IRS Code 3401
    b. Euro
    c. Import and Export Price Indices
    d. Equity capital market

17. _____ is money accepted for exchange of goods in an economy. The prevalence of one money over another arises, usually, when a government designates through decrees that the government shall accept only particular notes and coins in payment for taxes. Typically, money of _____ consists of stamped coins and minted paper bills.
    a. Security thread
    b. Local currency
    c. Totnes pound
    d. Currency

18. In economics, _____ is a sustained decrease in the general price level of goods and services. _____ occurs when the annual inflation rate falls below zero percent, resulting in an increase in the real value of money -- a negative inflation rate. This should not be confused with disinflation, a slow-down in the inflation rate (i.e. when the inflation decreases, but still remains positive.)

Chapter 1. A Tour of the World

a. Deflation
b. Tobit model
c. Price revolution
d. Literacy rate

19. The _____ is an American stock exchange. It is the largest electronic screen-based equity securities trading market in the United States. With approximately 3,800 companies, it has more trading volume per hour than any other stock exchange in the world.

a. Nasdaq
b. 100-year flood
c. 1921 recession
d. 130-30 fund

20. In economics and finance, _____ is the practice of taking advantage of a price differential between two or more markets: striking a combination of matching deals that capitalize upon the imbalance, the profit being the difference between the market prices. When used by academics, an _____ is a transaction that involves no negative cash flow at any probabilistic or temporal state and a positive cash flow in at least one state; in simple terms, a risk-free profit. A person who engages in _____ is called an arbitrageur--such as a bank or brokerage firm.

a. Electronic trading
b. Alternext
c. Options Price Reporting Authority
d. Arbitrage

21. _____ in economics and business is the result of an exchange and from that trade we assign a numerical monetary value to a good, service or asset. If Alice trades Bob 4 apples for an orange, the _____ of an orange is 4 apples. Inversely, the _____ of an apple is 1/4 oranges.

a. Price war
b. Premium pricing
c. Price book
d. Price

22. The _____ is a group of three respected economists who advise the President of the United States on economic policy. It is a part of the Executive Office of the President of the United States, and provides much of the economic policy of the White House. The council prepares the annual Economic Report of the President.

a. Council of Economic Advisers
b. Constrained Pareto optimality
c. Federal Reserve Bank Notes
d. Hybrid renewable energy systems

23. The _____ is an international organization that oversees the global financial system by following the macroeconomic policies of its member countries, in particular those with an impact on exchange rates and the balance of payments. It is an organization formed to stabilize international exchange rates and facilitate development. It also offers financial and technical assistance to its members, making it an international lender of last resort.

a. Office of Thrift Supervision
b. ACCRA Cost of Living Index
c. ACEA agreement
d. International Monetary Fund

24. _____ is a branch of applied statistics focusing on the collection, processing, compilation and dissemination of statistics concerning the economy of a region, a country or a group of countries. _____ is also referred as a subtopic of official statistics, since most of the _____ are produced by official organizations (e.g. statistical institutes, intergovernmental organizations such as United Nations, European Union or OECD, central banks, ministries, etc.). _____ provide the empirical data needed in economic research (econometrics) and they are the basis for decision and economic policy making.

a. Economic statistics
b. Event study
c. Indirect least squares
d. ACCRA Cost of Living Index

25. A variety of measures of national income and output are used in economics to estimate total economic activity in a country or region, including gross domestic product (GDP), _____ , and net national income (NNI.)

There are three main ways of calculating these numbers; the output approach, the income approach and the expenditure approach. In theory, the three must yield the same, because total expenditures on goods and services must equal the total income paid to the producers (GNI), and that must also equal the total value of the output of goods and services (_____.)

a. Purchasing power parity
b. Gross world product
c. Household final consumption expenditure
d. Gross national product

Chapter 2. A Tour of the Book

1. _____ is a misspelled phrase from Latin 'pro capite' phrase meaning per head with pro meaning 'per' or 'for each' and capite meaning 'head.' Both words together equate to the phrase 'for each head.'

It is usually used in the field of statistics to indicate the average per person for any given concern, such as income, crime rate, etc.

It is also used in wills to indicate that each of the named beneficiaries should receive, by devise or bequest, equal shares of the estate. This is in contrast to a per stirpes division, in which each branch of the inheriting family inherits an equal share of the estate.

 a. Sargan test
 b. Per capita
 c. False positive rate
 d. Population statistics

2. In economics _____s are goods that are ultimately consumed rather than used in the production of another good. For example, a car sold to a consumer is a _____; the components such as tires sold to the car manufacturer are not; they are intermediate goods used to make the _____.

When used in measures of national income and output the term _____s only includes new goods.

 a. Substitute good
 b. Luxury good
 c. Final good
 d. Goods and services

3. The _____ or gross domestic income (GDI), a basic measure of an economy's economic performance, is the market value of all final goods and services produced within the borders of a nation in a year. _____ can be defined in three ways, all of which are conceptually identical. First, it is equal to the total expenditures for all final goods and services produced within the country in a stipulated period of time (usually a 365-day year.)

 a. Gross domestic product
 b. Countercyclical
 c. Monopolistic competition
 d. Market structure

4. A _____ is an object whose consumption increases the utility of the consumer, for which the quantity demanded exceeds the quantity supplied at zero price. _____s are usually modeled as having diminishing marginal utility. The first individual purchase has high utility; the second has less.

 a. Good
 b. Merit good
 c. Pie method
 d. Composite good

5. A variety of measures of national income and output are used in economics to estimate total economic activity in a country or region, including gross domestic product (GDP), _____ , and net national income (NNI.)

There are three main ways of calculating these numbers; the output approach, the income approach and the expenditure approach. In theory, the three must yield the same, because total expenditures on goods and services must equal the total income paid to the producers (GNI), and that must also equal the total value of the output of goods and services (_____.)

 a. Household final consumption expenditure
 b. Gross national product
 c. Gross world product
 d. Purchasing power parity

Chapter 2. A Tour of the Book

6. _____ or producer goods are goods used as inputs in the production of other goods, such as partly finished goods. They are goods used in production of final goods. A firm may make then use _____, or make then sell, or buy then use them.

   a. Inflation adjustment
   b. Income distribution
   c. Economic forecasting
   d. Intermediate goods

7. A variety of measures of _____ and output are used in economics to estimate total economic activity in a country or region, including gross domestic product (GDP), gross national product (GNP), and net _____

There are three main ways of calculating these numbers; the output approach, the income approach and the expenditure approach. In theory, the three must yield the same, because total expenditures on goods and services must equal the total income paid to the producers (Gnational income), and that must also equal the total value of the output of goods and services (GNP.)

   a. National Income
   b. Volume index
   c. GNI per capita
   d. Gross world product

8. _____ use double-entry accounting to report the monetary value and sources of output produced in a country and the distribution of incomes that production generates. Data are available at the national and industry levels.

The NIPA summarizes national income on the left (debit, revenue) side and national product on the right (credit, expense) side of a two-column accounting report.

   a. Gross private domestic investment
   b. Net national product
   c. Current account
   d. National Income and Product Accounts

9. Economics:

   - _____, the desire to own something and the ability to pay for it
   - _____ curve, a graphic representation of a _____ schedule
   - _____ deposit, the money in checking accounts
   - _____ pull theory, the theory that inflation occurs when _____ for goods and services exceeds existing supplies
   - _____ schedule, a table that lists the quantity of a good a person will buy it each different price
   - _____ side economics, the school of economics at believes government spending and tax cuts open economy by raising _____

   a. McKesson ' Robbins scandal
   b. Demand
   c. Production
   d. Variability

10. In microeconomics, _____ is quite simply the conversion of inputs into outputs. It is an economic process that uses resources to create a good or service that is suitable for exchange. This can include manufacturing, storing, shipping, and packaging.

a. Solved
b. Red Guards
c. Production
d. MET

11. In financial accounting, the _____ is one of the accounts in shareholders' equity. Sole proprietorships have a single _____ in the owner's equity. Partnerships maintain a _____ for each of the partners.
   a. Compensation of employees
   b. Current account
   c. Net national product
   d. Capital account

12. _____ is the a method of technical and economic research of the systems for purpose to optimize a parity between system's consumer functions or properties and expenses to achieve those functions or properties.

This methodology for continuous perfection of production, industrial technologies, organizational structures was developed by Juryj Sobolev in 1948 at the 'Perm telephone factory'

- 1948 Juryj Sobolev - the first success in application of a method analysis at the 'Perm telephone factory' .
- 1949 - the first application for the invention as result of use of the new method.

Today in economically developed countries practically each enterprise or the company use methodology of the kind of functional-cost analysis as a practice of the quality management, most full satisfying to principles of standards of series ISO 9000.

- Interest of consumer not in products itself, but the advantage which it will receive from its usage.
- The consumer aspires to reduce his expenses
- Functions needed by consumer can be executed in the various ways, and, hence, with various efficiency and expenses. Among possible alternatives of realization of functions exist such in which the parity of quality and the price is the optimal for the consumer.

The goal of _____ is achievement of the highest consumer satisfaction of production at simultaneous decrease in all kinds of industrial expenses Classical _____ has three English synonyms - Value Engineering, Value Management, Value Analysis.

   a. Monopoly wage
   b. Function cost analysis
   c. Willingness to pay
   d. Staple financing

13. _____ refers to the additional value of a commodity over the cost of commodities used to produce it from the previous stage of production. An example is the price of gasoline at the pump over the price of the oil in it. In national accounts used in macroeconomics, it refers to the contribution of the factors of production, i.e., land, labor, and capital goods, to raising the value of a product and corresponds to the incomes received by the owners of these factors.
   a. Solow residual
   b. Value added
   c. Full employment
   d. Hodrick-Prescott filter

14. An _____, in economics, is the amount by which the real Gross domestic product exceeds potential GDP. The real GDP is also known as GDP 'adjusted for inflation', 'constant prices' GDP or 'constant dollar' GDP, because it measures the aggregate output in a country's income accounts in a given year, expressed in base-year prices. On the other hand, the potential GDP is the quantity of real GDP when a country's economy is at full-employment.

a. ACCRA Cost of Living Index
b. ACEA agreement
c. Inflationary gap
d. AD-IA Model

15. _____ is a macroeconomic measure of the size of an economy adjusted for price changes and inflation. It measures in constant prices the output of final goods and services and incomes within an economy. The formula for its definition is [(Nominal GDP)/(GDP deflator)] x 100, however, it is not calculated in this way.
   a. TED spread
   b. Bureau of Labor Statistics
   c. Gross world product
   d. Real Gross domestic product

16. _____ is the price of a commodity such as a good or service in terms of another; ie, the ratio of two prices. A _____ may be expressed in terms of a ratio between any two prices or the ratio between the price of one particular good and a weighted average of all other goods available in the market. A _____ is an opportunity cost.
   a. Relative price
   b. False shortage
   c. Food cooperative
   d. False economy

17. _____ in economics and business is the result of an exchange and from that trade we assign a numerical monetary value to a good, service or asset. If Alice trades Bob 4 apples for an orange, the _____ of an orange is 4 apples. Inversely, the _____ of an apple is 1/4 oranges.
   a. Price war
   b. Price book
   c. Premium pricing
   d. Price

18. _____ is a common concept in economics, and gives rise to derived concepts such as consumer debt. Generally _____ is defined by opposition to production. But the precise definition can vary because different schools of economists define production quite differently.
   a. Foreclosure data providers
   b. Consumption
   c. Cash or share options
   d. Federal Reserve Bank Notes

19. In economics, a _____ is a general slowdown in economic activity over a sustained period of time, or a business cycle contraction. During _____s, many macroeconomic indicators vary in a similar way. Production as measured by Gross Domestic Product (GDP), employment, investment spending, capacity utilization, household incomes and business profits all fall during _____s.
   a. Monetary economics
   b. Leading indicators
   c. Treasury View
   d. Recession

20. _____ is one of the four Ps of the marketing mix. The other three aspects are product, promotion, and place. It is also a key variable in microeconomic price allocation theory.
   a. Premium pricing
   b. Point of total assumption
   c. Pricing
   d. Guaranteed Maximum Price

21. In economics, the people in the _____ are the suppliers of labor. The _____ is all the nonmilitary people who are employed or unemployed. In 2005, the worldwide _____ was over 3 billion people.
   a. Labor force
   b. Grenelle agreements
   c. Distributed workforce
   d. Departmentalization

22. Unemployment occurs when a person is available to work and seeking work but currently without work. The prevalence of unemployment is usually measured using the _____, which is defined as the percentage of those in the labor force who are unemployed. The _____ is also used in economic studies and economic indexes such as the United States' Conference Board's Index of Leading Indicators as a measure of the state of the macroeconomics.
   a. ACCRA Cost of Living Index
   b. ACEA agreement
   c. AD-IA Model
   d. Unemployment rate

23. In economics, a _____ is a person of legal employment age who is not actively seeking employment. This is usually due to the fact that an individual has given up looking or has had no success in finding a job, hence the term 'discouraged.' Their belief may derive from a variety of factors including: a shortage of jobs in their locality or line of work; perceived discrimination for reasons such as age, race, sex and religion; a lack of necessary skills, training or experience; or, a chronic illness or disability. Some _____s, however, are voluntarily unemployed such as stay-at-home parents, pregnant mothers, and will beneficiaries.
   a. Hedonimetry
   b. Demand side economics
   c. Relative income hypothesis
   d. Discouraged worker

24. In economics, the _____ is a historical inverse relation between the rate of unemployment and the rate of inflation in an economy. Stated simply, the lower the unemployment in an economy, the higher the rate of increase in nominal wages in the economy. Rate of Change of Wages against Unemployment, United Kingdom 1913-1948 from Phillips (1958)

William Phillips, a New Zealand born economist, wrote a paper in 1958 titled The Relationship between Unemployment and the Rate of Change of Money Wages in the United Kingdom 1861-1957, which was published in the quarterly journal Economica.

   a. Phillips curve
   b. Lorenz curve
   c. Cost curve
   d. Demand curve

25. The _____ or black market is a market where all commerce is conducted without regard to taxation, law or regulations of trade. The term is also often known as the underdog, shadow economy, black economy, parallel economy or phantom trades.

In modern societies the _____ covers a vast array of activities.

   a. Information economy
   b. Autarky
   c. Information markets
   d. Underground economy

26. _____ is a broad label that refers to any individuals or households that use goods and services generated within the economy. The concept of a _____ is used in different contexts, so that the usage and significance of the term may vary.

Typically when business people and economists talk of _____s they are talking about person as _____, an aggregated commodity item with little individuality other than that expressed in the buy/not-buy decision.

a. 130-30 fund
b. 100-year flood
c. Consumer
d. 1921 recession

27. A _____ is a measure of the average price of consumer goods and services purchased by households. A _____ measures a price change for a constant market basket of goods and services from one period to the next within the same area (city, region, or nation.) It is a price index determined by measuring the price of a standard group of goods meant to represent the typical market basket of a typical urban consumer.
   a. Cost-of-living index
   b. Lipstick index
   c. CPI
   d. Consumer price index

28. In economics, _____ is a sustained decrease in the general price level of goods and services. _____ occurs when the annual inflation rate falls below zero percent, resulting in an increase in the real value of money -- a negative inflation rate. This should not be confused with disinflation, a slow-down in the inflation rate (i.e. when the inflation decreases, but still remains positive.)
   a. Price revolution
   b. Deflation
   c. Tobit model
   d. Literacy rate

29. An _____ is an economic data figure reflecting price or quantity compared with a standard or base value. The base usually equals 100 and the _____ is usually expressed as 100 times the ratio to the base value. For example, if a commodity costs twice as much in 1970 as it did in 1960, its _____ would be 200 relative to 1960.
   a. Index number
   b. International economics
   c. ACCRA Cost of Living Index
   d. Economic depreciation

30. In economics, _____ is a rise in the general level of prices of goods and services in an economy over a period of time. When the general price level rises, each unit of currency buys fewer goods and services; consequently, _____ is also a decline in the real value of money--a loss of purchasing power in the medium of exchange which is also the monetary unit of account in the economy. A chief measure of general price-level _____ is the general _____ rate, which is the percentage change in a general price index (normally the Consumer Price Index) over time.
   a. Inflation
   b. Energy economics
   c. Economic
   d. Opportunity cost

31. In economics, the _____ is a measure of inflation, the rate of increase of a price index (for example, a consumer price index.)It is the percentage rate of change in price level over time. The rate of decrease in the purchasing power of money is approximately equal.

It's used to calculate the real interest rate, as well as real increases in wages, and official measurements of this rate act as input variables to COLA adjustments and Inflation derivatives prices.

   a. Interest rate option
   b. Inflation rate
   c. Edgeworth paradox
   d. Equity value

32. A _____ is a normalized average (typically a weighted average) of prices for a given class of goods or services in a given region, during a given interval of time. It is a statistic designed to help to compare how these prices, taken as a whole, differ between time periods or geographical locations.

Price indices have several potential uses.

a. Product sabotage
b. Two-part tariff
c. Transactional Net Margin Method
d. Price index

33. A _____ is a hypothetical measure of overall prices for some set of goods and services, in a given region during a given interval, normalized relative to some base set. Typically, a _____ is approximated with a price index.

The classical dichotomy is the assumption that there is a relatively clean distinction between overall increases or decreases in prices and underlying, e;reale; economic variables.

a. Price level
b. Discretionary spending
c. Price elasticity of supply
d. Discouraged worker

34. In statistics, a _____ is a value that allows data to be measured over time in terms of some base period ussually through a price index in order to distinguish between changes in the money value of GNP which result from a change in prices and those which result from a change in physical output. It is the measure of the price level for some quantity. A _____ serves as a price index in which the effects of inflation are nulled.

a. Market microstructure
b. Deflator
c. Blanket order
d. Contingent employment

35. The _____, a unit of the United States Department of Labor, is the principal fact-finding agency for the U.S. government in the broad field of labor economics and statistics. The BLS is an independent national statistical agency that collects, processes, analyzes, and disseminates essential statistical data to the American public, the U.S. Congress, other Federal agencies, State and local governments, business, and labor representatives. The BLS also serves as a statistical resource to the Department of Labor.

a. Gross Regional Product
b. Bureau of Labor Statistics
c. Gross world product
d. Gross national product

36. _____ is the cost of maintaining a certain standard of living. Changes in the _____ over time are often operationalized in a _____ index. _____ calculations are also used to compare the cost of maintaining a certain standard of living in different geographic areas.

a. Cost of living
b. Bear raid
c. Restructuring
d. Decision process tool

37. A _____ measures average changes in prices received by domestic producers for their output. It is one of several price indices

Its importance is being undermined by the steady decline in manufactured goods as a share of spending.

A number of countries that now report a _____ previously reported a Wholesale Price Index.

a. Hemline index
b. Gross national product
c. Visible balance
d. Producer price index

38. The term _____s refers to wages that have been adjusted for inflation. This term is used in contrast to nominal wages or unadjusted wages.

The use of adjusted figures is in undertaking some form of economic analysis.

a. Real wage
c. Profit sharing
b. Federal Wage System
d. Living wage

39. In algebra, a _____ is a function depending on n that associates a scalar, det(A), to an n×n square matrix A. The fundamental geometric meaning of a _____ is a scale factor for measure when A is regarded as a linear transformation. _____s are important both in calculus, where they enter the substitution rule for several variables, and in multilinear algebra.

For a fixed nonnegative integer n, there is a unique _____ function for the n×n matrices over any commutative ring R. In particular, this function exists when R is the field of real or complex numbers.

a. 100-year flood
c. 1921 recession
b. 130-30 fund
d. Determinant

Chapter 3. The Goods Market

1. Economics:

   - _____, the desire to own something and the ability to pay for it
   - _____ curve, a graphic representation of a _____ schedule
   - _____ deposit, the money in checking accounts
   - _____ pull theory, the theory that inflation occurs when _____ for goods and services exceeds existing supplies
   - _____ schedule, a table that lists the quantity of a good a person will buy it each different price
   - _____ side economics, the school of economics at believes government spending and tax cuts open economy by raising _____

   a. Demand
   b. Variability
   c. McKesson ' Robbins scandal
   d. Production

2. In microeconomics, _____ is quite simply the conversion of inputs into outputs. It is an economic process that uses resources to create a good or service that is suitable for exchange. This can include manufacturing, storing, shipping, and packaging.

   a. Red Guards
   b. MET
   c. Solved
   d. Production

3. _____ is a common concept in economics, and gives rise to derived concepts such as consumer debt. Generally _____ is defined by opposition to production. But the precise definition can vary because different schools of economists define production quite differently.

   a. Cash or share options
   b. Foreclosure data providers
   c. Federal Reserve Bank Notes
   d. Consumption

4. The _____ or gross domestic income (GDI), a basic measure of an economy's economic performance, is the market value of all final goods and services produced within the borders of a nation in a year. _____ can be defined in three ways, all of which are conceptually identical. First, it is equal to the total expenditures for all final goods and services produced within the country in a stipulated period of time (usually a 365-day year.)

   a. Gross domestic product
   b. Market structure
   c. Countercyclical
   d. Monopolistic competition

5. In economics, an _____ is any good or commodity, transported from one country to another country in a legitimate fashion, typically for use in trade. _____ goods or services are provided to foreign consumers by domestic producers. _____ is an important part of international trade.

   a. ACEA agreement
   b. ACCRA Cost of Living Index
   c. AD-IA Model
   d. Export

6. _____ in economics refers to investment in fixed capital, i.e. tangible capital goods (real means of production or residential buildings), or to the replacement of depreciated capital goods.

Thus, _____ is investment in physical assets such as machinery, land, buildings, installations, vehicles, or technology. Normally, a company balance sheet will state both the amount of expenditure on fixed assets during the quarter or year, and the total value of the stock of fixed assets owned.

Chapter 3. The Goods Market

a. Deferred financing costs
c. Historical cost
b. Depreciation
d. Fixed investment

7. _____ or government expenditure is classified by economists into three main types. Government purchases of goods and services for current use are classed as government consumption. Government purchases of goods and services intended to create future benefits, such as infrastructure investment or research spending, are classed as government investment.
   a. 100-year flood
   c. 130-30 fund
   b. 1921 recession
   d. Government spending

8. In economics, an _____ is any good (e.g. a commodity) or service brought into one country from another country in a legitimate fashion, typically for use in trade. It is a good that is brought in from another country for sale. _____ goods or services are provided to domestic consumers by foreign producers. An _____ in the receiving country is an export to the sending country.
   a. Import quota
   c. Incoterms
   b. Economic integration
   d. Import

9. _____ relates to the composition of GDP. What is produced in a certain country is naturally also sold, but some of the goods produced in a given year may not be sold the same year, but in later years. Conversely, some of the goods sold in a given year might have been produced in an earlier year.
   a. Investment decisions
   c. Investment theory
   b. Obelisk International
   d. Inventory investment

10. The balance of trade (or net exports, sometimes symbolized as NX) is the difference between the monetary value of exports and imports in an economy over a certain period of time. It is the relationship between a nation's imports and exports. A favorable balance of trade is known as a trade surplus and consists of exporting more than is imported; an unfavorable balance of trade is known as a _____ or, informally, a trade gap.
    a. Trade deficit
    c. Computational economic
    b. Complementary asset
    d. Demographics of India

11. The balance of trade (or net exports, sometimes symbolized as NX) is the difference between the monetary value of exports and imports in an economy over a certain period of time. It is the relationship between a nation's imports and exports. A favorable balance of trade is known as a _____ and consists of exporting more than is imported; an unfavorable balance of trade is known as a trade deficit or, informally, a trade gap.
    a. Business valuation standards
    c. Trade surplus
    b. Dividend unit
    d. Black-Scholes

12. In economics, the _____ is a single mathematical function used to express consumer spending. It was developed by John Maynard Keynes and detailed most famously in his book The General Theory of Employment, Interest, and Money. The function is used to calculate the amount of total consumption in an economy.
    a. DAD-SAS model
    c. Procyclical
    b. Liquidity preference
    d. Consumption function

13. A _____ product is a product designed for cheapness and short-term convenience rather than medium to long-term durability, with most products only intended for single use. The term is also sometimes used for products that may last several months (ex. _____ air filters) to distinguish from similar products that last indefinitely (ex.

Chapter 3. The Goods Market

a. 1921 recession
c. 100-year flood
b. Disposable
d. 130-30 fund

14. _____ is gross income minus income tax on that income.

Discretionary income is income after subtracting taxes and normal expenses (such as rent or mortgage, utilities, insurance, medical, transportation, property maintenance, child support, inflation, food and sundries, 'c.) to maintain a certain standard of living.

a. Disposable personal income
c. Taxation as theft
b. Stamp Act
d. Disposable income

15. A _____ is an object whose consumption increases the utility of the consumer, for which the quantity demanded exceeds the quantity supplied at zero price. _____s are usually modeled as having diminishing marginal utility. The first individual purchase has high utility; the second has less.

a. Good
c. Merit good
b. Pie method
d. Composite good

16. In economics, the _____ is an empirical metric that quantifies induced consumption, the concept that the increase in personal consumer spending (consumption) that occurs with an increase in disposable income (income after taxes and transfers.) For example, if a household earns one extra dollar of disposable income, and the _____ is 0.65, then of that dollar, the household will spend 65 cents and save 35 cents.

Mathematically, the _____ (MPC) function is expressed as the derivative of the consumption (C) function with respect to disposable income (Y.)

a. Supply shock
c. Technology shock
b. Marginal propensity to consume
d. Marginal propensity to import

17. _____ refers to an action or object coming from outside a system. It is the opposite of endogenous, something generated from within the system.

- In an economic model, an _____ change is one that comes from outside the model and is unexplained by the model. For example, in the simple supply and demand model, a change in consumer tastes or preferences is unexplained by the model and also leads to endogenous changes in demand that lead to changes in the equilibrium price. Put another way, an _____ change involves an alteration of a variable that is autonomous, i.e., unaffected by the workings of the model.

- In linear regression, it means that the variable is independent of all other response values.

- In biology, '_____' refers to an action or object coming from the outside of a system. For example, an _____ contrast agent in medical imaging refers to a liquid injected into the patient intravenously that enhances visibility of a pathology, such as a tumor.

Chapter 3. The Goods Market

a. ACEA agreement
b. AD-IA Model
c. ACCRA Cost of Living Index
d. Exogenous

18. The term _____ refers to government debt, expenditures and revenues, or to finance (particularly financial revenue) in general.

- _____ deficit is the budget deficit of federal or local government
- _____ policy is the discretionary spending of governments. Contrasts with monetary policy.
- _____ year and _____ quarter are reporting periods for firms and other agencies.

a. Drawdown
b. Fiscal
c. Procter ' Gamble
d. Bucket shop

19. In economics, _____ is the use of government spending and revenue collection to influence the economy.

_____ can be contrasted with the other main type of economic policy, monetary policy, which attempts to stabilize the economy by controlling interest rates and the supply of money. The two main instruments of _____ are government spending and taxation.

a. 100-year flood
b. Sustainable investment rule
c. Fiscal policy
d. Fiscalism

20. To _____ is to impose a financial charge or other levy upon a taxpayer by a state or the functional equivalent of a state.

_____ es are also imposed by many subnational entities. _____ es consist of direct _____ or indirect _____, and may be paid in money or as its labour equivalent (often but not always unpaid.)

a. 1921 recession
b. 130-30 fund
c. 100-year flood
d. Tax

21. To tax is to impose a financial charge or other levy upon a taxpayer by a state or the functional equivalent of a state.

_____ are also imposed by many subnational entities. _____ consist of direct tax or indirect tax, and may be paid in money or as its labour equivalent (often but not always unpaid.)

a. 100-year flood
b. Taxes
c. 1921 recession
d. 130-30 fund

22. _____ is the a method of technical and economic research of the systems for purpose to optimize a parity between system's consumer functions or properties and expenses to achieve those functions or properties.

Chapter 3. The Goods Market

This methodology for continuous perfection of production, industrial technologies, organizational structures was developed by Juryj Sobolev in 1948 at the 'Perm telephone factory'

- 1948 Juryj Sobolev - the first success in application of a method analysis at the 'Perm telephone factory'.
- 1949 - the first application for the invention as result of use of the new method.

Today in economically developed countries practically each enterprise or the company use methodology of the kind of functional-cost analysis as a practice of the quality management, most full satisfying to principles of standards of series ISO 9000.

- Interest of consumer not in products itself, but the advantage which it will receive from its usage.
- The consumer aspires to reduce his expenses
- Functions needed by consumer can be executed in the various ways, and, hence, with various efficiency and expenses. Among possible alternatives of realization of functions exist such in which the parity of quality and the price is the optimal for the consumer.

The goal of _____ is achievement of the highest consumer satisfaction of production at simultaneous decrease in all kinds of industrial expenses Classical _____ has three English synonyms - Value Engineering, Value Management, Value Analysis.

a. Staple financing
c. Function cost analysis
b. Willingness to pay
d. Monopoly wage

23. _____ refers to the additional value of a commodity over the cost of commodities used to produce it from the previous stage of production. An example is the price of gasoline at the pump over the price of the oil in it. In national accounts used in macroeconomics, it refers to the contribution of the factors of production, i.e., land, labor, and capital goods, to raising the value of a product and corresponds to the incomes received by the owners of these factors.

a. Hodrick-Prescott filter
c. Full employment
b. Solow residual
d. Value added

24. In economics, economic equilibrium is simply a state of the world where economic forces are balanced and in the absence of external influences the (equilibrium) values of economic variables will not change. It is the point at which quantity demanded and quantity supplied are equal. _____, for example, refers to a condition where a market price is established through competition such that the amount of goods or services sought by buyers is equal to the amount of goods or services produced by sellers.

a. Regulated market
c. Product-Market Growth Matrix
b. Marketization
d. Market Equilibrium

25. _____ is a concept found in moral, political, and bioethical philosophy. Within these contexts, it refers to the capacity of a rational individual to make an informed, un-coerced decision. In moral and political philosophy, _____ is often used as the basis for determining moral responsibility for one's actions.

a. Autonomy
c. AD-IA Model
b. ACCRA Cost of Living Index
d. ACEA agreement

Chapter 3. The Goods Market

26. From a Keynesian point of view, a _____ in the public sector is achieved when the government equates the revenues with expenditure over the business cycles. In other words, a government's budget is balanced if its income is equal to its expenditure. It is a budget in which revenues are equal to spending.
    a. Budget theory
    b. Balanced budget
    c. Budget crisis
    d. Budget support

27. _____s is concerned with the tasks of developing and applying quantitative or statistical methods to the study and elucidation of economic principles. _____s combines economic theory with statistics to analyze and test economic relationships. Theoretical _____s considers questions about the statistical properties of estimators and tests, while applied _____s is concerned with the application of _____ methods to assess economic theories.
    a. Experimental economics
    b. Econometric
    c. Evolutionary economics
    d. Economic

28. _____ is a broad label that refers to any individuals or households that use goods and services generated within the economy. The concept of a _____ is used in different contexts, so that the usage and significance of the term may vary.

    Typically when business people and economists talk of _____s they are talking about person as _____, an aggregated commodity item with little individuality other than that expressed in the buy/not-buy decision.

    a. Consumer
    b. 100-year flood
    c. 130-30 fund
    d. 1921 recession

29. _____ is the degree of optimism that consumers feel about the overall state of the economy and their personal financial situation. How confident people feel about stability of their incomes determines their spending activity and therefore serves as one of the key indicators for the overall shape of the economy. In essence, if _____ is higher, consumers are making more purchases, boosting the economic expansion.
    a. Consumer behavior
    b. Communal marketing
    c. Consumer confidence
    d. Rule Developing Experimentation

30. In economics, a _____ is a general slowdown in economic activity over a sustained period of time, or a business cycle contraction. During _____s, many macroeconomic indicators vary in a similar way. Production as measured by Gross Domestic Product (GDP), employment, investment spending, capacity utilization, household incomes and business profits all fall during _____s.
    a. Leading indicators
    b. Monetary economics
    c. Treasury View
    d. Recession

31. The U.S. _____ is an indicator designed to measure consumer confidence, which is defined as the degree of optimism on the state of the economy that consumers are expressing through their activities of savings and spending. Global consumer confidence is not measured. Country by country analysis indicates huge variance around the globe.
    a. Constant dollars
    b. Cost-weighted activity index
    c. Rank mobility index
    d. Consumer confidence index

32. A _____ occurs when an entity spends more money than it takes in. The opposite of a _____ is a budget surplus. Debt is essentially an accumulated flow of deficits.

a. Funding body
c. Lump-sum tax
b. Public Financial Management
d. Budget deficit

33. A _____ is a situation in which the government takes in more than it spends.
a. Budget set
c. 130-30 fund
b. 100-year flood
d. Budget surplus

34. _____ is a fee paid on borrowed assets. It is the price paid for the use of borrowed money, or, money earned by deposited funds. Assets that are sometimes lent with _____ include money, shares, consumer goods through hire purchase, major assets such as aircraft, and even entire factories in finance lease arrangements.
a. Internal debt
c. Insolvency
b. Asset protection
d. Interest

35. _____, 1st Baron Keynes was a renowned economist from Britain whose many ideas on economic and political theories as well as on many governments' monetary policies influenced America. He advocated a government that played an active role in the lives of people regarding business, economy, etc. In this role, the government would use fiscal measures to reduce the consequences of recessions, economic depressions and booms.
a. Adolph Fischer
c. Adam Smith
b. Adolf Hitler
d. John Maynard Keynes

36. The _____ is the apparent contradiction that although water is on the whole more useful, in terms of survival, than diamonds, diamonds command a higher price in the market. The economist Adam Smith is often considered to be the classic presenter of this paradox. Nicolaus Copernicus, John Locke, John Law and others had previously tried to explain the disparity.
a. 100-year flood
c. St. Petersburg paradox
b. 130-30 fund
d. Paradox of value

Chapter 4. Financial Markets

1. _____ is an American economist and was the Chairman of the Federal Reserve of the United States from 1987 to 2006. He currently works as a private advisor and providing consulting for firms through his company, Greenspan Associates LLC.

First appointed Federal Reserve chairman by President Ronald Reagan in August 1987, he was reappointed at successive four-year intervals until retiring on January 31, 2006 after the second-longest tenure in the position.

   a. Alan Greenspan
   c. Adam Smith
   b. Adolph Fischer
   d. Adolf Hitler

2. In finance, a _____ is a debt security, in which the authorized issuer owes the holders a debt and, depending on the terms of the _____, is obliged to pay interest (the coupon) and/or to repay the principal at a later date, termed maturity. A _____ is a formal contract to repay borrowed money with interest at fixed intervals.

Thus a _____ is like a loan: the issuer is the borrower (debtor), the holder is the lender (creditor), and the coupon is the interest.

   a. Callable
   c. Zero-coupon
   b. Prize Bond
   d. Bond

3. A _____, reserve bank, or monetary authority is the entity responsible for the monetary policy of a country or of a group of member states. It is a bank that can lend money to other banks in times of need. Its primary responsibility is to maintain the stability of the national currency and money supply, but more active duties include controlling subsidized-loan interest rates, and acting as a lender of last resort to the banking sector during times of financial crisis (private banks often being integral to the national financial system.)
   a. Central bank
   c. 100-year flood
   b. 130-30 fund
   d. 1921 recession

4. _____ is money accepted for exchange of goods in an economy. The prevalence of one money over another arises, usually, when a government designates through decrees that the government shall accept only particular notes and coins in payment for taxes. Typically, money of _____ consists of stamped coins and minted paper bills.
   a. Totnes pound
   c. Local currency
   b. Security thread
   d. Currency

5. Economics:

   - _____,the desire to own something and the ability to pay for it
   - _____ curve,a graphic representation of a _____ schedule
   - _____ deposit, the money in checking accounts
   - _____ pull theory,the theory that inflation occurs when _____ for goods and services exceeds existing supplies
   - _____ schedule,a table that lists the quantity of a good a person will buy it each different price
   - _____ side economics,the school of economics at believes government spending and tax cuts open economy by raising _____

Chapter 4. Financial Markets

a. Production
b. Variability
c. McKesson ' Robbins scandal
d. Demand

6. The _____ is the desired holding of money balances in the form of cash or bank deposits.

Money is dominated as store of value by interest bearing assets. However, money is necessary to carry out transactions, or in other words, it provides liquidity.

a. Borrowing base
b. Market neutral
c. Conglomerate merger
d. Demand for money

7. In finance, the _____ is the global financial market for short-term borrowing and lending. It provides short-term liquidity funding for the global financial system. The _____ is where short-term obligations such as Treasury bills, commercial paper and bankers' acceptances are bought and sold.

a. Consignment stock
b. T-Model
c. Deferred compensation
d. Money market

8. The _____ or gross domestic income (GDI), a basic measure of an economy's economic performance, is the market value of all final goods and services produced within the borders of a nation in a year. _____ can be defined in three ways, all of which are conceptually identical. First, it is equal to the total expenditures for all final goods and services produced within the country in a stipulated period of time (usually a 365-day year.)

a. Monopolistic competition
b. Market structure
c. Gross domestic product
d. Countercyclical

9. In economics, a _____ is a mechanism that allows people to easily buy and sell (trade) financial securities (such as stocks and bonds), commodities (such as precious metals or agricultural goods), and other fungible items of value at low transaction costs and at prices that reflect the efficient-market hypothesis.

_____s have evolved significantly over several hundred years and are undergoing constant innovation to improve liquidity.

Both general markets (where many commodities are traded) and specialized markets (where only one commodity is traded) exist.

a. Convertible arbitrage
b. Noise trader
c. Market anomaly
d. Financial market

10. _____ is a fee paid on borrowed assets. It is the price paid for the use of borrowed money , or, money earned by deposited funds . Assets that are sometimes lent with _____ include money, shares, consumer goods through hire purchase, major assets such as aircraft, and even entire factories in finance lease arrangements.

a. Insolvency
b. Internal debt
c. Asset protection
d. Interest

11. An _____ is the price a borrower pays for the use of money they do not own, for instance a small company might borrow from a bank to kick start their business, and the return a lender receives for deferring the use of funds, by lending it to the borrower. _____s are normally expressed as a percentage rate over the period of one year.

Chapter 4. Financial Markets

_____s targets are also a vital tool of monetary policy and are used to control variables like investment, inflation, and unemployment.

a. Arrow-Debreu model
c. Enterprise value
b. ACCRA Cost of Living Index
d. Interest rate

12. Market _____ is a business, economics or investment term that refers to an asset's ability to be easily converted through an act of buying or selling without causing a significant movement in the price and with minimum loss of value. Money, or cash on hand, is the most liquid asset. An act of exchange of a less liquid asset with a more liquid asset is called liquidation.

a. 130-30 fund
c. 100-year flood
b. 1921 recession
d. Liquidity

13. _____, in economics, is the quantity of money measured in a particular currency and is directly proportional to the price level.

This means, among other things, that if the price level rises by 10%, 10% more money than before is necessary in order to maintain stability. For example, if it costs $20 to buy an item, and the price level increases by 10%, the dollar amount necessary to buy the item increases by 10% (in this case by $2), which brings the total cost of the item to $22.

a. Money of account
c. Silver Thursday
b. Nominal money
d. Limping bimetallism

14. In economics, the _____ measures the payments that flow between any individual country and all other countries. It is used to summarize all international economic transactions for that country during a specific time period, usually a year. The _____ is determined by the country's exports and imports of goods, services, and financial capital, as well as financial transfers.

a. Gross world product
c. Skyscraper Index
b. Gross domestic product per barrel
d. Balance of payments

15. A _____ is the transfer of wealth from one party (such as a person or company) to another. A _____ is usually made in exchange for the provision of goods, services or both, or to fulfill a legal obligation.

The simplest and oldest form of _____ is barter, the exchange of one good or service for another.

a. Going concern
c. Social gravity
b. Payment
d. Soft count

16. The _____ is the average frequency with which a unit of money is spent in a specific period of time. Velocity associates the amount of economic activity associated with a given money supply. When the period is understood, the velocity may be present as a pure number; otherwise it should be given as a pure number over time.

a. Velocity of money
c. Money supply
b. Chartalism
d. Neutrality of money

Chapter 4. Financial Markets

17. _____ is the process by which the government, central bank (ii) availability of money, and (iii) cost of money or rate of interest, in order to attain a set of objectives oriented towards the growth and stability of the economy. Monetary theory provides insight into how to craft optimal _____.

_____ is referred to as either being an expansionary policy where an expansionary policy increases the total supply of money in the economy, and a contractionary policy decreases the total money supply.

- a. Monetary policy
- b. 1921 recession
- c. 100-year flood
- d. 130-30 fund

18. _____ refers to the objective and subjective components of the believability of a source or message.

Traditionally, _____ has two key components: trustworthiness and expertise, which both have objective and subjective components. Trustworthiness is a based more on subjective factors, but can include objective measurements such as established reliability.

- a. 130-30 fund
- b. 100-year flood
- c. 1921 recession
- d. Credibility

19. In economics, the _____ is the term used to refer to the environment in which bonds are bought and sold between a central bank ' its regulated banks. It is not a free market process.

- To intervene in the 'business cycle', a central bank may choose to go into the _____ and buy or sell government bonds, which is known as _____ operations to increase reserves.

- a. Open market
- b. Inside money
- c. ACCRA Cost of Living Index
- d. Outside money

20. _____ are the means of implementing monetary policy by which a central bank controls its national money supply by buying and selling government securities, or other financial instruments. Monetary targets, such as interest rates or exchange rates, are used to guide this implementation.

Since most money is now in the form of electronic records, rather than paper records such as banknotes, _____ are conducted simply by electronically increasing or decreasing ('crediting' or 'debiting') the amount of money that a bank has, e.g., in its reserve account at the central bank, in exchange for a bank selling or buying a financial instrument.

- a. AD-IA Model
- b. Open market operations
- c. ACCRA Cost of Living Index
- d. ACEA agreement

21. A United States Treasury security is a government debt issued by the United States Department of the Treasury through the Bureau of the Public Debt. Treasury securities are the debt financing instruments of the United States Federal government, and they are often referred to simply as Treasuries. There are four types of marketable treasury securities: _____, Treasury notes, Treasury bonds, and Treasury Inflation Protected Securities (TIPS.)

a. Labour battalions	b. Treasury bills
c. Debt to Assets	d. Lawcards

22. _____ in economics and business is the result of an exchange and from that trade we assign a numerical monetary value to a good, service or asset. If Alice trades Bob 4 apples for an orange, the _____ of an orange is 4 apples. Inversely, the _____ of an apple is 1/4 oranges.

a. Premium pricing	b. Price war
c. Price book	d. Price

23. In economics, _____ is the total amount of money available in an economy at a particular point in time. There are several ways to define 'money', but standard measures usually include currency in circulation and demand deposits.

_____ data are recorded and published, usually by the government or the central bank of the country.

a. Neutrality of money	b. Velocity of money
c. Veil of money	d. Money supply

24. In financial accounting, a _____ or statement of financial position is a summary of a person's or organization's balances. Assets, liabilities and ownership equity are listed as of a specific date, such as the end of its financial year. A _____ is often described as a snapshot of a company's financial condition.

a. 1921 recession	b. Balance sheet
c. 130-30 fund	d. 100-year flood

25. The cost advantages of using _____ include:

- Reconciling conflicting preferences of lenders and borrowers

- Risk aversion- intermediaries help spread out and decrease the risks

- Economies of scale- using _____ reduces the costs of lending and borrowing

- Economies of scope- intermediaries concentrate on the demands of the lenders and borrowers and are able to enhance their products and services (use same inputs to produce different outputs)

_____ include:

- Banks
- Building societies
- Credit unions
- Financial advisers or brokers
- Insurance companies
- Collective investment schemes
- Pension funds

Financial institutions (intermediaries) perform the vital role of bringing together those economic agents with surplus funds who want to lend, with those with a shortage of funds who want to borrow.

In doing this they offer the major benefits of maturity and risk transformation. It is possible for this to be done by direct contact between the ultimate borrowers, but there are major cost disadvantages of direct finance.

Indeed, one explanation of the existence of specialist _____ is that they have a related (cost) advantage in offering financial services, which not only enables them to make profit, but also raises the overall efficiency of the economy.

   a. SICAV
   c. Collective investment scheme
   b. Broker-dealer
   d. Financial intermediaries

26. The reserve requirement (or required _____) is a bank regulation that sets the minimum reserves each bank must hold to customer deposits and notes. It would normally be in the form of fiat currency stored in a bank vault (vault cash), or with a central bank.

The _____ is sometimes used as a tool in the monetary policy, influencing the country's economy, borrowing, and interest rates.

   a. First player wins
   c. Bank-State-Branch
   b. Dividend unit
   d. Reserve ratio

27. A _____ is an expression that compares quantities relative to each other. The most common examples involve two quantities, but any number of quantities can be compared. _____s are represented mathematically by separating each quantity with a colon, for example the _____ 2:3, which is read as the _____ 'two to three'.
   a. Y-intercept
   c. 130-30 fund
   b. Ratio
   d. 100-year flood

28. _____ is an economic model based on price, utility and quantity in a market. It predicts that in a competitive market, price will function to equalize the quantity demanded by consumers, and the quantity supplied by producers, resulting in an economic equilibrium of price and quantity. The model incorporates other factors changing equilibrium as a shift of demand and/or supply.
   a. Deferred gratification
   c. Rational addiction
   b. Joint demand
   d. Supply and demand

29. A _____ occurs when a large number of bank customers withdraw their deposits because they believe the bank is insolvent. As a _____ progresses, it generates its own momentum, in a kind of self-fulfilling prophecy: as more people withdraw their deposits, the likelihood of default increases, and this encourages further withdrawals. This can destabilize the bank to the point where it faces bankruptcy.
   a. Funds Transfer Pricing
   c. Tier 1 capital
   b. Bank run
   d. Fractional-reserve banking

30. _____ is a proposed type of bank called a narrow bank also called a safe bank. Ultimately, if adopted widely, this could lead to an entirely new banking system. Narrow banks can, by risk reduction measures designed into the narrow bank, significantly reduce potential bank runs and the need for a deposit insurance provided by the central bank.
   a. Global ATM Alliance
   b. Diamond-Dybvig model
   c. Repo Rate
   d. Narrow banking

31. _____, in law and economics, is a form of risk management primarily used to hedge against the risk of a contingent loss. _____ is defined as the equitable transfer of the risk of a loss, from one entity to another, in exchange for a premium, and can be thought of as a guaranteed small loss to prevent a large, possibly devastating loss. An insurer is a company selling the _____; an insured or policyholder is the person or entity buying the _____.
   a. AD-IA Model
   b. Insurance
   c. ACEA agreement
   d. ACCRA Cost of Living Index

32. In the United States, _____ are overnight borrowings by banks to maintain their bank reserves at the Federal Reserve. Banks keep reserves at Federal Reserve Banks to meet their reserve requirements and to clear financial transactions. Transactions in the _____ market enable depository institutions with reserve balances in excess of reserve requirements to lend reserves to institutions with reserve deficiencies.
   a. Federal funds
   b. Federal Reserve Transparency Act
   c. Federal funds rate
   d. Term auction facility

33. In the United States, the _____ is the interest rate at which private depository institutions (mostly banks) lend balances (federal funds) at the Federal Reserve to other depository institutions, usually overnight. It is the interest rate banks charge each other for loans. Changing the target rate is one way the Chairman of the Federal Reserve can influence the supply of money in the U.S. economy..
   a. Federal banking
   b. Federal funds rate
   c. Monetary Policy Report to the Congress
   d. Term auction facility

34. _____ is a macroeconomic term referring to the monetary base -- that is, to highly liquid money and includes currency and vault cash. In the United States, with the beginning of the Federal Reserve System in 1913, _____ also includes deposit liabilities of the Federal Reserve System to banks.

The monetary base is typically controlled by the institution in a country that controls monetary policy.

   a. Rational expectations
   b. Complex multiplier
   c. Hodrick-Prescott filter
   d. High-powered money

35. In economics, the _____ is a term relating to the money supply, the amount of money in the economy. The _____ comprises only coins, paper money, and commercial banks' reserves with the central bank. Broader measures of the money supply include the public's bank deposits .
   a. Chartalism
   b. Monetary economy
   c. Quantum economics
   d. Monetary base

36. The most common mechanism used to measure this increase in the money supply is typically called the _____. It calculates the maximum amount of money that an initial deposit can be expanded to with a given reserve ratio - such a factor is called a multiplier.

Chapter 4. Financial Markets

The _____, m, is the inverse of the reserve requirement, R:

$$m = \frac{1}{R}$$

This formula stems from the fact that the sum of the 'amount loaned out' column above can be expressed mathematically as a geometric series with a common ratio of 1 − R.

a. Fixed-income arbitrage
b. Money multiplier
c. Flow to Equity-Approach
d. Kibbutz volunteers

Chapter 5. Goods and Financial Markets: The IS-LM Model

1. _____ is a fee paid on borrowed assets. It is the price paid for the use of borrowed money , or, money earned by deposited funds . Assets that are sometimes lent with _____ include money, shares, consumer goods through hire purchase, major assets such as aircraft, and even entire factories in finance lease arrangements.
   a. Asset protection
   b. Internal debt
   c. Insolvency
   d. Interest

2. _____, 1st Baron Keynes was a renowned economist from Britain whose many ideas on economic and political theories as well as on many governments' monetary policies influenced America. He advocated a government that played an active role in the lives of people regarding business, economy, etc. In this role, the government would use fiscal measures to reduce the consequences of recessions, economic depressions and booms.
   a. Adolph Fischer
   b. Adam Smith
   c. John Maynard Keynes
   d. Adolf Hitler

3. In economics, _____ is the total demand for final goods and services in the economy (Y) at a given time and price level. It is the amount of goods and services in the economy that will be purchased at all possible price levels. This is the demand for the gross domestic product of a country when inventory levels are static.
   a. Aggregate expenditure
   b. Aggregation problem
   c. Aggregate supply
   d. Aggregate demand

4. Economics:

   - _____,the desire to own something and the ability to pay for it
   - _____ curve,a graphic representation of a _____ schedule
   - _____ deposit, the money in checking accounts
   - _____ pull theory,the theory that inflation occurs when _____ for goods and services exceeds existing supplies
   - _____ schedule,a table that lists the quantity of a good a person will buy it each different price
   - _____ side economics,the school of economics at believes government spending and tax cuts open economy by raising _____

   a. Demand
   b. Variability
   c. McKesson ' Robbins scandal
   d. Production

5. A _____ is an object whose consumption increases the utility of the consumer, for which the quantity demanded exceeds the quantity supplied at zero price. _____s are usually modeled as having diminishing marginal utility. The first individual purchase has high utility; the second has less.
   a. Merit good
   b. Pie method
   c. Good
   d. Composite good

6. An _____ is the price a borrower pays for the use of money they do not own, for instance a small company might borrow from a bank to kick start their business, and the return a lender receives for deferring the use of funds, by lending it to the borrower. _____s are normally expressed as a percentage rate over the period of one year.

   _____s targets are also a vital tool of monetary policy and are used to control variables like investment, inflation, and unemployment.

Chapter 5. Goods and Financial Markets: The IS-LM Model

a. Interest rate
b. Arrow-Debreu model
c. ACCRA Cost of Living Index
d. Enterprise value

7. The _____ or gross domestic income (GDI), a basic measure of an economy's economic performance, is the market value of all final goods and services produced within the borders of a nation in a year. _____ can be defined in three ways, all of which are conceptually identical. First, it is equal to the total expenditures for all final goods and services produced within the country in a stipulated period of time (usually a 365-day year.)

a. Gross domestic product
b. Countercyclical
c. Market structure
d. Monopolistic competition

8. _____, in economics, is the quantity of money measured in a particular currency and is directly proportional to the price level.

This means, among other things, that if the price level rises by 10%, 10% more money than before is necessary in order to maintain stability. For example, if it costs $20 to buy an item, and the price level increases by 10%, the dollar amount necessary to buy the item increases by 10% (in this case by $2), which brings the total cost of the item to $22.

a. Nominal money
b. Silver Thursday
c. Money of account
d. Limping bimetallism

9. _____ is the income of individuals or nations after adjusting for inflation. It is calculated by subtracting inflation from the nominal income. Real variables, such as _____, real GDP, and real interest rate are variables that are measured in physical units, while nominal variables such as nominal income, nominal GDP, and nominal interest rate are measured in monetary units.

a. Windfall gain
b. Net national income
c. Family income
d. Real income

10. An _____, in economics, is the amount by which the real Gross domestic product exceeds potential GDP. The real GDP is also known as GDP 'adjusted for inflation', 'constant prices' GDP or 'constant dollar' GDP, because it measures the aggregate output in a country's income accounts in a given year, expressed in base-year prices. On the other hand, the potential GDP is the quantity of real GDP when a country's economy is at full-employment.

a. ACEA agreement
b. Inflationary gap
c. ACCRA Cost of Living Index
d. AD-IA Model

11. The term _____ refers to government debt, expenditures and revenues, or to finance (particularly financial revenue) in general.

- _____ deficit is the budget deficit of federal or local government
- _____ policy is the discretionary spending of governments. Contrasts with monetary policy.
- _____ year and _____ quarter are reporting periods for firms and other agencies.

Chapter 5. Goods and Financial Markets: The IS-LM Model

a. Procter ' Gamble
b. Drawdown
c. Fiscal
d. Bucket shop

12. In economics, _____ is the use of government spending and revenue collection to influence the economy.

_____ can be contrasted with the other main type of economic policy, monetary policy, which attempts to stabilize the economy by controlling interest rates and the supply of money. The two main instruments of _____ are government spending and taxation.

a. Sustainable investment rule
b. 100-year flood
c. Fiscalism
d. Fiscal policy

13. To _____ is to impose a financial charge or other levy upon a taxpayer by a state or the functional equivalent of a state.

_____es are also imposed by many subnational entities. _____es consist of direct _____ or indirect _____, and may be paid in money or as its labour equivalent (often but not always unpaid.)

a. 130-30 fund
b. 1921 recession
c. 100-year flood
d. Tax

14. To tax is to impose a financial charge or other levy upon a taxpayer by a state or the functional equivalent of a state.

_____ are also imposed by many subnational entities. _____ consist of direct tax or indirect tax, and may be paid in money or as its labour equivalent (often but not always unpaid.)

a. 100-year flood
b. 1921 recession
c. Taxes
d. 130-30 fund

15. _____ is the process by which the government, central bank (ii) availability of money, and (iii) cost of money or rate of interest, in order to attain a set of objectives oriented towards the growth and stability of the economy. Monetary theory provides insight into how to craft optimal _____.

_____ is referred to as either being an expansionary policy where an expansionary policy increases the total supply of money in the economy, and a contractionary policy decreases the total money supply.

a. 130-30 fund
b. 100-year flood
c. Monetary policy
d. 1921 recession

16. _____ refers to the objective and subjective components of the believability of a source or message.

Traditionally, _____ has two key components: trustworthiness and expertise, which both have objective and subjective components. Trustworthiness is a based more on subjective factors, but can include objective measurements such as established reliability.

a. 100-year flood
b. 1921 recession
c. 130-30 fund
d. Credibility

17. _____s is the social science that studies the production, distribution, and consumption of goods and services. The term _____s comes from the Ancient Greek oá¼°κονομῖα from oá¼¶κος (oikos, 'house') + νÏŒμος (nomos, 'custom' or 'law'), hence 'rules of the house(hold)'. Current _____ models developed out of the broader field of political economy in the late 19th century, owing to a desire to use an empirical approach more akin to the physical sciences.
   a. Opportunity cost
   b. Inflation
   c. Energy economics
   d. Economic

18. _____ is an American economist and was the Chairman of the Federal Reserve of the United States from 1987 to 2006. He currently works as a private advisor and providing consulting for firms through his company, Greenspan Associates LLC.

First appointed Federal Reserve chairman by President Ronald Reagan in August 1987, he was reappointed at successive four-year intervals until retiring on January 31, 2006 after the second-longest tenure in the position.

   a. Adam Smith
   b. Alan Greenspan
   c. Adolph Fischer
   d. Adolf Hitler

19. The _____ is a US private, nonprofit research organization dedicated to studying the science and empirics of economics, especially the American economy. It is 'committed to undertaking and disseminating unbiased economic research among public policymakers, business professionals, and the academic community.' It publishes NBER Working Papers and books. The NBER is located in Cambridge, Massachusetts with branch offices in Palo Alto, California, and New York City.
   a. Deutsche Bank
   b. Non-governmental organization
   c. National Bureau of Economic Research
   d. CEFTA

20. In economics, a _____ is a general slowdown in economic activity over a sustained period of time, or a business cycle contraction. During _____s, many macroeconomic indicators vary in a similar way. Production as measured by Gross Domestic Product (GDP), employment, investment spending, capacity utilization, household incomes and business profits all fall during _____s.
   a. Monetary economics
   b. Recession
   c. Leading indicators
   d. Treasury View

21. _____ is a misspelled phrase from Latin 'pro capite' phrase meaning per head with pro meaning 'per' or 'for each' and capite meaning 'head.' Both words together equate to the phrase 'for each head.'

It is usually used in the field of statistics to indicate the average per person for any given concern, such as income, crime rate, etc.

It is also used in wills to indicate that each of the named beneficiaries should receive, by devise or bequest, equal shares of the estate. This is in contrast to a per stirpes division, in which each branch of the inheriting family inherits an equal share of the estate.

a. False positive rate
b. Per capita
c. Sargan test
d. Population statistics

Chapter 6. The Labor Market

1. In economics, the people in the _____ are the suppliers of labor. The _____ is all the nonmilitary people who are employed or unemployed. In 2005, the worldwide _____ was over 3 billion people.
   a. Grenelle agreements
   b. Departmentalization
   c. Labor force
   d. Distributed workforce

2. Unemployment occurs when a person is available to work and seeking work but currently without work. The prevalence of unemployment is usually measured using the _____, which is defined as the percentage of those in the labor force who are unemployed. The _____ is also used in economic studies and economic indexes such as the United States' Conference Board's Index of Leading Indicators as a measure of the state of the macroeconomics.
   a. Unemployment rate
   b. ACEA agreement
   c. ACCRA Cost of Living Index
   d. AD-IA Model

3. _____ is the temporary suspension or permanent termination of employment of an employee or (more commonly) a group of employees for business reasons, such as the decision that certain positions are no longer necessary or a business slow-down or interruption in work. Originally the term '_____' referred exclusively to a temporary interruption in work, as when factory work cyclically falls off. However, in recent times the term can also refer to the permanent elimination of a position.
   a. Retirement
   b. Termination of employment
   c. 100-year flood
   d. Layoff

4. In economics, a _____ is a person of legal employment age who is not actively seeking employment. This is usually due to the fact that an individual has given up looking or has had no success in finding a job, hence the term 'discouraged.' Their belief may derive from a variety of factors including: a shortage of jobs in their locality or line of work; perceived discrimination for reasons such as age, race, sex and religion; a lack of necessary skills, training or experience; or, a chronic illness or disability. Some _____s, however, are voluntarily unemployed such as stay-at-home parents, pregnant mothers, and will beneficiaries.
   a. Relative income hypothesis
   b. Hedonimetry
   c. Demand side economics
   d. Discouraged worker

5. In finance, the _____ of a financial asset measures the sensitivity of the asset's price to interest rate movements. There are various definitions of _____ and derived quantities, discussed below. If not otherwise specified, '_____' generally means the Macaulay _____, as defined below.
   a. 100-year flood
   b. Time value of money
   c. Duration
   d. Newtonian time

6. The _____ is an economic and political union of 27 member states, located primarily in Europe. It was established by the Treaty of Maastricht on 1 November 1993, upon the foundations of the pre-existing European Economic Community. With a population of almost 500 million, the _____ generates an estimated 30% share (US$18.4 trillion in 2008) of the nominal gross world product.
   a. European Court of Justice
   b. European Union
   c. ACEA agreement
   d. ACCRA Cost of Living Index

7. A _____ is a group of people who share or are motivated by at least one common issue or interest, or work together on a specific project(s) to achieve a common objective. _____s are also characterised by attempts to share and exercise political and social power and to make decisions on a consensus-driven and egalitarian basis. _____s differ from cooperatives in that they are not necessarily focused upon an economic benefit or saving (but can be that as well).

a. 130-30 fund
b. Collective
c. 100-year flood
d. 1921 recession

8. In organized labor, _____ is the method whereby workers organize together (usually in unions) to meet, converse, and negotiate upon the work conditions with their employers normally resulting in a written contract setting forth the wages, hours, and other conditions to be observed for a stipulated period.It is the practice in which union and company representatives meet to negotiate a new labor contract. In various national labor and employment law contexts, _____ takes on a more specific legal meaning and so, in a broad sense, however, it is the coming together of workers to negotiate their employment.

A collective agreement is a labor contract between an employer and one or more unions.

a. Collective bargaining
b. Designated Suppliers Program
c. Demarcation dispute
d. Strikebreaker

9. In labor economics, the _____ is the lowest wage rate at which a worker would be willing to accept a particular type of job. A job offer involving the same type of work and the same working conditions, but at a lower wage rate, would be rejected by the worker.

An individual's _____ may change over time depending on a number of factors, like changes in the individual's overall wealth, changes in marital status or living arrangements, length of unemployment, and health and disability issues.

a. Minsky moment
b. Dematerialization
c. Reservation wage
d. Stylized fact

10. In labor economics, the _____ hypothesis argues that wages, at least in some markets, are determined by more than simply supply and demand. Specifically, it points to the incentive for managers to pay their employees more than the market-clearing wage in order to increase their productivity or efficiency. This increased labor productivity pays for the relatively higher wages.

a. Inflatable rats
b. Earnings calls
c. Exogenous growth model
d. Efficiency wage

11. _____ was the American founder of the Ford Motor Company and father of modern assembly lines used in mass production. His introduction of the Model T automobile revolutionized transportation and American industry. He was a prolific inventor and was awarded 161 U.S. patents.

a. Maximilian Carl Emil Weber
b. George Cabot Lodge II
c. Werner Sombart
d. Henry Ford

12. In economics, the _____ is a historical inverse relation between the rate of unemployment and the rate of inflation in an economy. Stated simply, the lower the unemployment in an economy, the higher the rate of increase in nominal wages in the economy. Rate of Change of Wages against Unemployment, United Kingdom 1913-1948 from Phillips (1958)

William Phillips, a New Zealand born economist, wrote a paper in 1958 titled The Relationship between Unemployment and the Rate of Change of Money Wages in the United Kingdom 1861-1957, which was published in the quarterly journal Economica.

a. Lorenz curve
b. Cost curve
c. Phillips curve
d. Demand curve

13. _____ in economics and business is the result of an exchange and from that trade we assign a numerical monetary value to a good, service or asset. If Alice trades Bob 4 apples for an orange, the _____ of an orange is 4 apples. Inversely, the _____ of an apple is 1/4 oranges.

a. Premium pricing
b. Price war
c. Price book
d. Price

14. _____, in law and economics, is a form of risk management primarily used to hedge against the risk of a contingent loss. _____ is defined as the equitable transfer of the risk of a loss, from one entity to another, in exchange for a premium, and can be thought of as a guaranteed small loss to prevent a large, possibly devastating loss. An insurer is a company selling the _____; an insured or policyholder is the person or entity buying the _____.

a. Insurance
b. ACCRA Cost of Living Index
c. AD-IA Model
d. ACEA agreement

15. A _____ is a hypothetical measure of overall prices for some set of goods and services, in a given region during a given interval, normalized relative to some base set. Typically, a _____ is approximated with a price index.

The classical dichotomy is the assumption that there is a relatively clean distinction between overall increases or decreases in prices and underlying, e;reale; economic variables.

a. Discretionary spending
b. Price level
c. Price elasticity of supply
d. Discouraged worker

16. Wisconsin originated the idea of _____ in the U.S. in 1932. In the United States, there are 50 state _____ programs plus one each in the District of Columbia and Puerto Rico. Through the Social Security Act of 1935, the Federal Government of the United States effectively coerced the individual states into adopting _____ plans.

a. AD-IA Model
b. ACCRA Cost of Living Index
c. Unemployment insurance
d. ACEA agreement

17. In economics, the _____ functional form of production functions is widely used to represent the relationship of an output to inputs. It was proposed by Knut Wicksell (1851-1926), and tested against statistical evidence by Charles Cobb and Paul Douglas in 1900-1928.

For production, the function is

$$Y = AL^{\alpha}K^{\beta},$$

where:

- Y = total production (the monetary value of all goods produced in a year)
- L = labor input
- K = capital input
- A = total factor productivity
- α and β are the output elasticities of labor and capital, respectively. These values are constants determined by available technology.

Output elasticity measures the responsiveness of output to a change in levels of either labor or capital used in production, ceteris paribus. For example if α = 0.15, a 1% increase in labor would lead to approximately a 0.15% increase in output.

a. Cobb-Douglas
b. Growth accounting
c. Social savings
d. Demand-pull theory

18. In microeconomics, _____ is quite simply the conversion of inputs into outputs. It is an economic process that uses resources to create a good or service that is suitable for exchange. This can include manufacturing, storing, shipping, and packaging.
a. Red Guards
b. Solved
c. MET
d. Production

19. In economics, a _____ is a function that specifies the output of a firm, an industry, or an entire economy for all combinations of inputs. A meta-_____ compares the practice of the existing entities converting inputs X into output y to determine the most efficient practice _____ of the existing entities, whether the most efficient feasible practice production or the most efficient actual practice production. In either case, the maximum output of a technologically-determined production process is a mathematical function of input factors of production.
a. Post-Fordism
b. Short-run
c. Constant elasticity of substitution
d. Production function

20. _____ in economics refers to metrics and measures of output from production processes, per unit of input. Labor _____, for example, is typically measured as a ratio of output per labor-hour, an input. _____ may be conceived of as a metrics of the technical or engineering efficiency of production.
a. Fordism
b. Production-possibility frontier
c. Productivity
d. Piece work

21. The _____ is a concept of economic activity developed in particular by Milton Friedman and Edmund Phelps in the 1960s, both recipients of the Nobel prize in economics. In both cases, the development of the concept is cited as a main motivation behind the prize. It represents the hypothetical unemployment rate consistent with aggregate production being at the 'long-run' level.
a. Robertson lag
b. Natural rate of unemployment
c. Romer Model
d. Real Business Cycle Theory

22. The term _____s refers to wages that have been adjusted for inflation. This term is used in contrast to nominal wages or unadjusted wages.

The use of adjusted figures is in undertaking some form of economic analysis.

a. Profit sharing
c. Living wage

b. Federal Wage System
d. Real wage

Chapter 7. Putting All Markets Together: The AS-AD Model

1. In economics, _____ is the total supply of goods and services produced by a national economy during a specific time period. It is the total amount of goods and services in the economy available at all possible price levels.
   a. Aggregation problem
   b. Aggregate supply
   c. Aggregate expenditure
   d. Aggregate demand

2. In economics, _____ is the total demand for final goods and services in the economy (Y) at a given time and price level. It is the amount of goods and services in the economy that will be purchased at all possible price levels. This is the demand for the gross domestic product of a country when inventory levels are static.
   a. Aggregation problem
   b. Aggregate supply
   c. Aggregate expenditure
   d. Aggregate demand

3. Economics:

   - _____ ,the desire to own something and the ability to pay for it
   - _____ curve, a graphic representation of a _____ schedule
   - _____ deposit, the money in checking accounts
   - _____ pull theory, the theory that inflation occurs when _____ for goods and services exceeds existing supplies
   - _____ schedule, a table that lists the quantity of a good a person will buy it each different price
   - _____ side economics, the school of economics at believes government spending and tax cuts open economy by raising _____

   a. Demand
   b. McKesson ' Robbins scandal
   c. Production
   d. Variability

4. A _____ is a public market for the trading of company stock and derivatives at an agreed price; these are securities listed on a stock exchange as well as those only traded privately.

   The size of the world _____ was estimated at about $36.6 trillion US at the beginning of October 2008. The total world derivatives market has been estimated at about $791 trillion face or nominal value, 11 times the size of the entire world economy.

   a. Adam Smith
   b. Adolf Hitler
   c. Adolph Fischer
   d. Stock market

5. _____ is a fee paid on borrowed assets. It is the price paid for the use of borrowed money, or, money earned by deposited funds. Assets that are sometimes lent with _____ include money, shares, consumer goods through hire purchase, major assets such as aircraft, and even entire factories in finance lease arrangements.
   a. Internal debt
   b. Insolvency
   c. Asset protection
   d. Interest

6. An _____ is the price a borrower pays for the use of money they do not own, for instance a small company might borrow from a bank to kick start their business, and the return a lender receives for deferring the use of funds, by lending it to the borrower. _____ s are normally expressed as a percentage rate over the period of one year.

_____s targets are also a vital tool of monetary policy and are used to control variables like investment, inflation, and unemployment.

a. ACCRA Cost of Living Index
b. Arrow-Debreu model
c. Enterprise value
d. Interest rate

7. _____ is the process by which the government, central bank (ii) availability of money, and (iii) cost of money or rate of interest, in order to attain a set of objectives oriented towards the growth and stability of the economy. Monetary theory provides insight into how to craft optimal _____.

_____ is referred to as either being an expansionary policy where an expansionary policy increases the total supply of money in the economy, and a contractionary policy decreases the total money supply.

a. 1921 recession
b. Monetary policy
c. 100-year flood
d. 130-30 fund

8. _____ refers to the objective and subjective components of the believability of a source or message.

Traditionally, _____ has two key components: trustworthiness and expertise, which both have objective and subjective components. Trustworthiness is a based more on subjective factors, but can include objective measurements such as established reliability.

a. 100-year flood
b. 1921 recession
c. Credibility
d. 130-30 fund

9. _____ is monetary policy that seeks to increase the size of the money supply. In most nations, monetary policy is controlled by either a central bank or a finance ministry

Neoclassical and Keynesian economics significantly differ on the effects and effectiveness of monetary policy on influencing the real economy; there is no clear consensus on how monetary policy affects real economic variables (aggregate output or income, employment.) Both economic schools accept that monetary policy affects monetary variables (price levels, interest rates.)

a. ACCRA Cost of Living Index
b. Expansionary Monetary policy
c. AD-IA Model
d. ACEA agreement

10. A _____ occurs when an entity spends more money than it takes in. The opposite of a _____ is a budget surplus. Debt is essentially an accumulated flow of deficits.
a. Public Financial Management
b. Funding body
c. Lump-sum tax
d. Budget deficit

Chapter 7. Putting All Markets Together: The AS-AD Model

11. A _____, reserve bank, or monetary authority is the entity responsible for the monetary policy of a country or of a group of member states. It is a bank that can lend money to other banks in times of need. Its primary responsibility is to maintain the stability of the national currency and money supply, but more active duties include controlling subsidized-loan interest rates, and acting as a lender of last resort to the banking sector during times of financial crisis (private banks often being integral to the national financial system.)
   a. 1921 recession
   b. 130-30 fund
   c. Central bank
   d. 100-year flood

12. Later Keynesians economists took up the notion and redefined it in terms that ignored the microeconomic time structure of production. On this later definition, _____ is the idea that a change in the stock of money affects only nominal variables in the economy such as prices, wages and exchange rates but no effect on real (inflation-adjusted) variables, like employment, real GDP, and real consumption. It is an important idea in classical economics and is related to the classical dichotomy.
   a. Neutrality of money
   b. Chartalism
   c. Veil of money
   d. Monetary reform

13. In finance, a _____ is a debt security, in which the authorized issuer owes the holders a debt and, depending on the terms of the _____, is obliged to pay interest (the coupon) and/or to repay the principal at a later date, termed maturity. A _____ is a formal contract to repay borrowed money with interest at fixed intervals.

    Thus a _____ is like a loan: the issuer is the borrower (debtor), the holder is the lender (creditor), and the coupon is the interest.

   a. Prize Bond
   b. Callable
   c. Zero-coupon
   d. Bond

14. _____ is a decrease in the rate of inflation. This phase of the business cycle, in which retailers can no longer pass on higher prices to their customers, often occurs during a recession. In contrast, deflation occurs when prices are actually dropping.
   a. Reflation
   b. Disinflation
   c. Stealth inflation
   d. Mundell-Tobin effect

15. In economics, _____ is a sustained decrease in the general price level of goods and services. _____ occurs when the annual inflation rate falls below zero percent, resulting in an increase in the real value of money -- a negative inflation rate. This should not be confused with disinflation, a slow-down in the inflation rate (i.e. when the inflation decreases, but still remains positive.)
   a. Literacy rate
   b. Deflation
   c. Tobit model
   d. Price revolution

16. _____ in economics and business is the result of an exchange and from that trade we assign a numerical monetary value to a good, service or asset. If Alice trades Bob 4 apples for an orange, the _____ of an orange is 4 apples. Inversely, the _____ of an apple is 1/4 oranges.
   a. Price
   b. Price book
   c. Premium pricing
   d. Price war

Chapter 7. Putting All Markets Together: The AS-AD Model

17. The _____ is an economic and political union of 27 member states, located primarily in Europe. It was established by the Treaty of Maastricht on 1 November 1993, upon the foundations of the pre-existing European Economic Community. With a population of almost 500 million, the _____ generates an estimated 30% share (US$18.4 trillion in 2008) of the nominal gross world product.
 a. European Court of Justice
 b. ACEA agreement
 c. ACCRA Cost of Living Index
 d. European Union

18. _____ is an economic situation in which inflation and economic stagnation occur simultaneously and remain unchecked for a period of time. The portmanteau _____ is generally attributed to British politician Iain Macleod, who coined the term in a speech to Parliament in 1965. The concept is notable partly because, in postwar macroeconomic theory, inflation and recession were regarded as mutually exclusive, and also because _____ has generally proven to be difficult and costly to eradicate once it gets started.
 a. Chronic inflation
 b. Price/wage spiral
 c. Stagflation
 d. Real interest rate

19. In economics, the concept of the _____ refers to the decision-making time frame of a firm in which at least one factor of production is fixed. Costs which are fixed in the _____ have no impact on a firms decisions. For example a firm can raise output by increasing the amount of labour through overtime.
 a. Product Pipeline
 b. Short-run
 c. Hicks-neutral technical change
 d. Productivity model

20. The term _____ refers to economy-wide fluctuations in production or economic activity over several months or years. These fluctuations occur around a long-term growth trend, and typically involve shifts over time between periods of relatively rapid economic growth (expansion or boom), and periods of relative stagnation or decline (contraction or recession.)

These fluctuations are often measured using the growth rate of real gross domestic product.

 a. Consumer theory
 b. Tobit model
 c. Nominal value
 d. Business cycle

21. In economics, a _____ is a general slowdown in economic activity over a sustained period of time, or a business cycle contraction. During _____s, many macroeconomic indicators vary in a similar way. Production as measured by Gross Domestic Product (GDP), employment, investment spending, capacity utilization, household incomes and business profits all fall during _____s.
 a. Monetary economics
 b. Leading indicators
 c. Recession
 d. Treasury View

22. A _____ is an event that suddenly changes the price of a commodity or service. It may be caused by a sudden increase or decrease in the supply of a particular good. This sudden change affects the equilibrium price.
 a. Supply shock
 b. Friedman rule
 c. SIMIC
 d. Demand shock

Chapter 8. The Natural Rate of Unemployment and the Phillips Curve

1. In economics, the _____ is a historical inverse relation between the rate of unemployment and the rate of inflation in an economy. Stated simply, the lower the unemployment in an economy, the higher the rate of increase in nominal wages in the economy. Rate of Change of Wages against Unemployment, United Kingdom 1913-1948 from Phillips (1958)

   William Phillips, a New Zealand born economist, wrote a paper in 1958 titled The Relationship between Unemployment and the Rate of Change of Money Wages in the United Kingdom 1861-1957, which was published in the quarterly journal Economica.

   a. Demand curve
   b. Lorenz curve
   c. Cost curve
   d. Phillips curve

2. _____ is a decrease in the rate of inflation. This phase of the business cycle, in which retailers can no longer pass on higher prices to their customers, often occurs during a recession. In contrast, deflation occurs when prices are actually dropping.
   a. Stealth inflation
   b. Mundell-Tobin effect
   c. Reflation
   d. Disinflation

3. The _____ is an economic and political union of 27 member states, located primarily in Europe. It was established by the Treaty of Maastricht on 1 November 1993, upon the foundations of the pre-existing European Economic Community. With a population of almost 500 million, the _____ generates an estimated 30% share (US$18.4 trillion in 2008) of the nominal gross world product.
   a. ACCRA Cost of Living Index
   b. European Court of Justice
   c. ACEA agreement
   d. European Union

4. In economics, _____ is inflation that is very high or 'out of control', a condition in which prices increase rapidly as a currency loses its value. Definitions used by the media vary from a cumulative inflation rate over three years approaching 100% to 'inflation exceeding 50% a month.' In informal usage the term is often applied to much lower rates. As a rule of thumb, normal inflation is reported per year, but _____ is often reported for much shorter intervals, often per month.
   a. 130-30 fund
   b. 100-year flood
   c. Hyperinflation
   d. 1921 recession

5. In economics, _____ is a rise in the general level of prices of goods and services in an economy over a period of time. When the general price level rises, each unit of currency buys fewer goods and services; consequently, _____ is also a decline in the real value of money--a loss of purchasing power in the medium of exchange which is also the monetary unit of account in the economy. A chief measure of general price-level _____ is the general _____ rate, which is the percentage change in a general price index (normally the Consumer Price Index) over time.
   a. Inflation
   b. Economic
   c. Opportunity cost
   d. Energy economics

6. The _____ was a worldwide economic downturn starting in most places in 1929 and ending at different times in the 1930s or early 1940s for different countries. It was the largest and most important economic depression in the 20th century, and is used in the 21st century as an example of how far the world's economy can fall. The _____ originated in the United States; historians most often use as a starting date the stock market crash on October 29, 1929, known as Black Tuesday.
   a. Great Depression
   b. Wall Street Crash of 1929
   c. Jarrow March
   d. British Empire Economic Conference

7. _____ was an American economist, statistician and public intellectual, and a recipient of the Nobel Memorial Prize in Economic Sciences. He is best known among scholars for his theoretical and empirical research, especially consumption analysis, monetary history and theory, and for his demonstration of the complexity of stabilization policy. A global public followed his restatement of a political philosophy that insisted on minimizing the role of government in favor of the private sector.
   a. Milton Friedman
   b. Adolf Hitler
   c. Adolph Fischer
   d. Adam Smith

8. The _____ is a concept of economic activity developed in particular by Milton Friedman and Edmund Phelps in the 1960s, both recipients of the Nobel prize in economics. In both cases, the development of the concept is cited as a main motivation behind the prize. It represents the hypothetical unemployment rate consistent with aggregate production being at the 'long-run' level.
   a. Romer Model
   b. Natural rate of unemployment
   c. Robertson lag
   d. Real Business Cycle Theory

9. In economics, the _____ is a measure of inflation, the rate of increase of a price index (for example, a consumer price index.)It is the percentage rate of change in price level over time. The rate of decrease in the purchasing power of money is approximately equal.

It's used to calculate the real interest rate, as well as real increases in wages, and official measurements of this rate act as input variables to COLA adjustments and Inflation derivatives prices.

   a. Interest rate option
   b. Inflation rate
   c. Equity value
   d. Edgeworth paradox

10. _____ is a technique to adjust income payments by means of a price index, in order to maintain the purchasing power of the public after inflation.

Applying a cost-of-living escalation COLA clause to a stream of periodic payments protects the real value of those payments and effectively transfers the risk of inflation from the payee to the payor, who must pay more each year to reflect the increases in prices. Thus, inflation _____ is often applied to pension payments, rents and other situations which are not subject to regular re-pricing in the market.

   a. Investment protection
   b. Indexation
   c. Ask price
   d. Interest rate parity

11. _____, 1st Baron Keynes was a renowned economist from Britain whose many ideas on economic and political theories as well as on many governments' monetary policies influenced America. He advocated a government that played an active role in the lives of people regarding business, economy, etc. In this role, the government would use fiscal measures to reduce the consequences of recessions, economic depressions and booms.
   a. Adolph Fischer
   b. John Maynard Keynes
   c. Adam Smith
   d. Adolf Hitler

12. In economics, _____ is a sustained decrease in the general price level of goods and services. _____ occurs when the annual inflation rate falls below zero percent, resulting in an increase in the real value of money -- a negative inflation rate. This should not be confused with disinflation, a slow-down in the inflation rate (i.e. when the inflation decreases, but still remains positive.)
   a. Tobit model
   b. Price revolution
   c. Literacy rate
   d. Deflation

Chapter 9. Inflation, Activity, and Nominal Money Growth

1. In economics, _____ is the total demand for final goods and services in the economy (Y) at a given time and price level. It is the amount of goods and services in the economy that will be purchased at all possible price levels. This is the demand for the gross domestic product of a country when inventory levels are static.
   a. Aggregation problem
   b. Aggregate supply
   c. Aggregate expenditure
   d. Aggregate demand

2. _____ is a decrease in the rate of inflation. This phase of the business cycle, in which retailers can no longer pass on higher prices to their customers, often occurs during a recession. In contrast, deflation occurs when prices are actually dropping.
   a. Reflation
   b. Disinflation
   c. Mundell-Tobin effect
   d. Stealth inflation

3. In economics, _____ is inflation that is very high or 'out of control', a condition in which prices increase rapidly as a currency loses its value. Definitions used by the media vary from a cumulative inflation rate over three years approaching 100% to 'inflation exceeding 50% a month.' In informal usage the term is often applied to much lower rates. As a rule of thumb, normal inflation is reported per year, but _____ is often reported for much shorter intervals, often per month.
   a. 100-year flood
   b. 1921 recession
   c. Hyperinflation
   d. 130-30 fund

4. _____, in economics, is the quantity of money measured in a particular currency and is directly proportional to the price level.

This means, among other things, that if the price level rises by 10%, 10% more money than before is necessary in order to maintain stability. For example, if it costs $20 to buy an item, and the price level increases by 10%, the dollar amount necessary to buy the item increases by 10% (in this case by $2), which brings the total cost of the item to $22.

   a. Silver Thursday
   b. Nominal money
   c. Limping bimetallism
   d. Money of account

5. In economics, the _____ is a historical inverse relation between the rate of unemployment and the rate of inflation in an economy. Stated simply, the lower the unemployment in an economy, the higher the rate of increase in nominal wages in the economy. Rate of Change of Wages against Unemployment, United Kingdom 1913-1948 from Phillips (1958)

William Phillips, a New Zealand born economist, wrote a paper in 1958 titled The Relationship between Unemployment and the Rate of Change of Money Wages in the United Kingdom 1861-1957, which was published in the quarterly journal Economica.

   a. Lorenz curve
   b. Demand curve
   c. Cost curve
   d. Phillips curve

Chapter 9. Inflation, Activity, and Nominal Money Growth

6. Economics:

    - _____, the desire to own something and the ability to pay for it
    - _____ curve, a graphic representation of a _____ schedule
    - _____ deposit, the money in checking accounts
    - _____ pull theory, the theory that inflation occurs when _____ for goods and services exceeds existing supplies
    - _____ schedule, a table that lists the quantity of a good a person will buy it each different price
    - _____ side economics, the school of economics at believes government spending and tax cuts open economy by raising _____

    a. Demand
    b. Production
    c. McKesson ' Robbins scandal
    d. Variability

7. In economics, _____ is a rise in the general level of prices of goods and services in an economy over a period of time. When the general price level rises, each unit of currency buys fewer goods and services; consequently, _____ is also a decline in the real value of money--a loss of purchasing power in the medium of exchange which is also the monetary unit of account in the economy. A chief measure of general price-level _____ is the general _____ rate, which is the percentage change in a general price index (normally the Consumer Price Index) over time.

    a. Opportunity cost
    b. Economic
    c. Energy economics
    d. Inflation

8. A _____, reserve bank, or monetary authority is the entity responsible for the monetary policy of a country or of a group of member states. It is a bank that can lend money to other banks in times of need. Its primary responsibility is to maintain the stability of the national currency and money supply, but more active duties include controlling subsidized-loan interest rates, and acting as a lender of last resort to the banking sector during times of financial crisis (private banks often being integral to the national financial system.)

    a. 100-year flood
    b. 1921 recession
    c. 130-30 fund
    d. Central bank

9. In finance, a _____ is a debt security, in which the authorized issuer owes the holders a debt and, depending on the terms of the _____, is obliged to pay interest (the coupon) and/or to repay the principal at a later date, termed maturity. A _____ is a formal contract to repay borrowed money with interest at fixed intervals.

    Thus a _____ is like a loan: the issuer is the borrower (debtor), the holder is the lender (creditor), and the coupon is the interest.

    a. Bond
    b. Callable
    c. Zero-coupon
    d. Prize Bond

10. _____ refers to the objective and subjective components of the believability of a source or message.

    Traditionally, _____ has two key components: trustworthiness and expertise, which both have objective and subjective components. Trustworthiness is a based more on subjective factors, but can include objective measurements such as established reliability.

a. 130-30 fund
c. 1921 recession
b. 100-year flood
d. Credibility

11. In finance, the _____ of a financial asset measures the sensitivity of the asset's price to interest rate movements. There are various definitions of _____ and derived quantities, discussed below. If not otherwise specified, '_____' generally means the Macaulay _____, as defined below.
    a. 100-year flood
    c. Duration
    b. Newtonian time
    d. Time value of money

12. A _____ is an expression that compares quantities relative to each other. The most common examples involve two quantities, but any number of quantities can be compared. _____s are represented mathematically by separating each quantity with a colon, for example the _____ 2:3, which is read as the _____ 'two to three'.
    a. 100-year flood
    c. 130-30 fund
    b. Ratio
    d. Y-intercept

13. The _____ says that it is naïve to try to predict the effects of a change in economic policy entirely on the basis of relationships observed in historical data, especially highly aggregated historical data.

The basic idea pre-dates Lucas's contribution, but in a 1976 paper he drove home the point that this simple notion invalidated policy advice based on conclusions drawn from estimated system of equation models. Because the parameters of those models were not structural - that is, not policy-invariant - they would necessarily change whenever policy - the rules of the game - was changed.

    a. Peak-load pricing
    c. Dahrendorf hypothesis
    b. Lucas critique
    d. Demand management

14. _____ is the process by which the government, central bank (ii) availability of money, and (iii) cost of money or rate of interest, in order to attain a set of objectives oriented towards the growth and stability of the economy. Monetary theory provides insight into how to craft optimal _____.

_____ is referred to as either being an expansionary policy where an expansionary policy increases the total supply of money in the economy, and a contractionary policy decreases the total money supply.

    a. Monetary policy
    c. 100-year flood
    b. 1921 recession
    d. 130-30 fund

15. _____s is the social science that studies the production, distribution, and consumption of goods and services. The term _____s comes from the Ancient Greek oá¼°κονομῖα from oá¼¶κος (oikos, 'house') + vĺŒμος (nomos, 'custom' or 'law'), hence 'rules of the house(hold)'. Current _____ models developed out of the broader field of political economy in the late 19th century, owing to a desire to use an empirical approach more akin to the physical sciences.
    a. Opportunity cost
    c. Energy economics
    b. Inflation
    d. Economic

Chapter 10. The Facts of Growth

1. The Organisation for Economic Co-operation and Development (_____) is an international organisation of 30 countries that accept the principles of representative democracy and free-market economy. Most _____ members are high-income economies with a high HDI and are regarded as developed countries.

    It originated in 1948 as the Organisation for European Economic Co-operation , led by Robert Marjolin of France, to help administer the Marshall Plan for the reconstruction of Europe after World War II.

    a. ACCRA Cost of Living Index
    b. AD-IA Model
    c. OECD
    d. ACEA agreement

2. _____ is generally measured by standards such as real (i.e. inflation adjusted) income per person and poverty rate. Other measures such as access and quality of health care, income growth inequality and educational standards are also used. Examples are access to certain goods (such as number of refrigerators per 1000 people), or measures of health such as life expectancy.
    a. Standard of living
    b. 130-30 fund
    c. Remuneration
    d. 100-year flood

3. _____ is a misspelled phrase from Latin 'pro capite' phrase meaning per head with pro meaning 'per' or 'for each' and capite meaning 'head.' Both words together equate to the phrase 'for each head.'

    It is usually used in the field of statistics to indicate the average per person for any given concern, such as income, crime rate, etc.

    It is also used in wills to indicate that each of the named beneficiaries should receive, by devise or bequest, equal shares of the estate. This is in contrast to a per stirpes division, in which each branch of the inheriting family inherits an equal share of the estate.

    a. Population statistics
    b. Sargan test
    c. False positive rate
    d. Per capita

4. _____ refers to a business or organization attempting to acquire goods or services to accomplish the goals of the enterprise. Though there are several organizations that attempt to set standards in the _____ process, processes can vary greatly between organizations. Typically the word '_____' is not used interchangeably with the word 'procurement', since procurement typically includes Expediting, Supplier Quality, and Traffic and Logistics (T'L) in addition to _____.
    a. 100-year flood
    b. Free port
    c. 130-30 fund
    d. Purchasing

5. _____ is the number of goods/services that can be purchased with a unit of currency. For example, if you had taken one dollar to a store in the 1950s, you would have been able to buy a greater number of items than you would today, indicating that you would have had a greater _____ in the 1950s. Currency can be either a commodity money, like gold or silver, or fiat currency like US dollars.
    a. Human Poverty Index
    b. Compliance cost
    c. Genuine progress indicator
    d. Purchasing power

6. The _____ theory uses the long-term equilibrium exchange rate of two currencies to equalize their purchasing power. Developed by Gustav Cassel in 1920, it is based on the law of one price: the theory states that, in ideally efficient markets, identical goods should have only one price.

Chapter 10. The Facts of Growth

This purchasing power SEM rate equalizes the purchasing power of different currencies in their home countries for a given basket of goods.

a. Measures of national income and output
b. Gross national product
c. Bureau of Labor Statistics
d. Purchasing power parity

7. The concept of _____ was originally used in the context of economic growth theories and industrial-organization innovation studies with specific focus on competition among firms. It is based on Joseph Schumpeter's notion of e;gales of creative destructione;. The hypothesis proposes that companies holding monopolies based on incumbent technologies have less incentive to innovate than potential rivals, and therefore they eventually lose their technological leadership role when new radical technological innovations are adopted by new firms which are ready to take the risks.

a. Suits index
b. Frisch elasticity of labor supply
c. Leapfrogging
d. Structural adjustment loan

8. In microeconomics, _____ is quite simply the conversion of inputs into outputs. It is an economic process that uses resources to create a good or service that is suitable for exchange. This can include manufacturing, storing, shipping, and packaging.

a. Red Guards
b. Production
c. MET
d. Solved

9. In economics, a _____ is a function that specifies the output of a firm, an industry, or an entire economy for all combinations of inputs. A meta-_____ compares the practice of the existing entities converting inputs X into output y to determine the most efficient practice _____ of the existing entities, whether the most efficient feasible practice production or the most efficient actual practice production. In either case, the maximum output of a technologically-determined production process is a mathematical function of input factors of production.

a. Constant elasticity of substitution
b. Post-Fordism
c. Short-run
d. Production function

10. In economics, _____ and economies of scale are related terms that describe what happens as the scale of production increases. They are different terms and should not be used interchangeably.

_____ refers to a technical property of production that examines changes in output subsequent to a proportional change in all inputs (where all inputs increase by a constant factor.)

a. Returns to scale
b. Customer equity
c. Necessity good
d. Constant returns to scale

11. In financial accounting, the _____ is one of the accounts in shareholders' equity. Sole proprietorships have a single _____ in the owner's equity. Partnerships maintain a _____ for each of the partners.

a. Compensation of employees
b. Current account
c. Net national product
d. Capital account

12. In economics, accounting and Marxian economics, _____ is often equated with investment of profit income, especially in real capital goods. The concentration and centralisation of capital are two of the results of such accumulation

Chapter 10. The Facts of Growth

But _____ can refer variously to

- working and consuming less than earned
- relying on the effects of compound interest to increase initial capital
- real investment in tangible means of production.
- financial investment in assets represented on paper.
- investment in non-productive physical assets such as residential real estate that appreciate in value.
- consuming less than produced by productive assets like farm land--saving or accumulating the residual
- 'human _____,' i.e., new education and training increasing the skills of the labour force.

Non-financial and financial _____ is usually needed for economic growth, since additional production usually requires additional funds to enlarge the scale of production. Smarter and more productive organization of production can also increase production without increased capital.

a. Marxian economics
c. Cultural Marxism

b. Capital accumulation
d. Productive force

Chapter 11. Saving, Capital Accumulation, and Output

1. In financial accounting, the _____ is one of the accounts in shareholders' equity. Sole proprietorships have a single _____ in the owner's equity. Partnerships maintain a _____ for each of the partners.
    a. Current account
    b. Net national product
    c. Compensation of employees
    d. Capital account

2. The _____ or gross domestic income (GDI), a basic measure of an economy's economic performance, is the market value of all final goods and services produced within the borders of a nation in a year. _____ can be defined in three ways, all of which are conceptually identical. First, it is equal to the total expenditures for all final goods and services produced within the country in a stipulated period of time (usually a 365-day year.)
    a. Market structure
    b. Countercyclical
    c. Gross domestic product
    d. Monopolistic competition

3. In economics, accounting and Marxian economics, _____ is often equated with investment of profit income, especially in real capital goods. The concentration and centralisation of capital are two of the results of such accumulation

    But _____ can refer variously to

    - working and consuming less than earned
    - relying on the effects of compound interest to increase initial capital
    - real investment in tangible means of production.
    - financial investment in assets represented on paper.
    - investment in non-productive physical assets such as residential real estate that appreciate in value.
    - consuming less than produced by productive assets like farm land--saving or accumulating the residual
    - 'human _____,' i.e., new education and training increasing the skills of the labour force.

    Non-financial and financial _____ is usually needed for economic growth, since additional production usually requires additional funds to enlarge the scale of production. Smarter and more productive organization of production can also increase production without increased capital.

    a. Productive force
    b. Marxian economics
    c. Cultural Marxism
    d. Capital accumulation

4. In economics, the _____ functional form of production functions is widely used to represent the relationship of an output to inputs. It was proposed by Knut Wicksell (1851-1926), and tested against statistical evidence by Charles Cobb and Paul Douglas in 1900-1928.

    For production, the function is

    $Y = AL^{\alpha}K^{\beta}$,

Chapter 11. Saving, Capital Accumulation, and Output

where:

- Y = total production (the monetary value of all goods produced in a year)
- L = labor input
- K = capital input
- A = total factor productivity
- α and β are the output elasticities of labor and capital, respectively. These values are constants determined by available technology.

Output elasticity measures the responsiveness of output to a change in levels of either labor or capital used in production, ceteris paribus. For example if α = 0.15, a 1% increase in labor would lead to approximately a 0.15% increase in output.

a. Cobb-Douglas
b. Social savings
c. Demand-pull theory
d. Growth accounting

5. In microeconomics, _____ is quite simply the conversion of inputs into outputs. It is an economic process that uses resources to create a good or service that is suitable for exchange. This can include manufacturing, storing, shipping, and packaging.

a. Red Guards
b. Solved
c. Production
d. MET

6. In economics, a _____ is a function that specifies the output of a firm, an industry, or an entire economy for all combinations of inputs. A meta-_____ compares the practice of the existing entities converting inputs X into output y to determine the most efficient practice _____ of the existing entities, whether the most efficient feasible practice production or the most efficient actual practice production. In either case, the maximum output of a technologically-determined production process is a mathematical function of input factors of production.

a. Production function
b. Post-Fordism
c. Short-run
d. Constant elasticity of substitution

7. The Organisation for Economic Co-operation and Development (_____) is an international organisation of 30 countries that accept the principles of representative democracy and free-market economy. Most _____ members are high-income economies with a high HDI and are regarded as developed countries.

It originated in 1948 as the Organisation for European Economic Co-operation, led by Robert Marjolin of France, to help administer the Marshall Plan for the reconstruction of Europe after World War II.

a. ACEA agreement
b. ACCRA Cost of Living Index
c. OECD
d. AD-IA Model

8. _____ is a common concept in economics, and gives rise to derived concepts such as consumer debt. Generally _____ is defined by opposition to production. But the precise definition can vary because different schools of economists define production quite differently.

a. Cash or share options
b. Federal Reserve Bank Notes
c. Foreclosure data providers
d. Consumption

9. _____ refers to the stock of skills and knowledge embodied in the ability to perform labor so as to produce economic value. It is the skills and knowledge gained by a worker through education and experience. Many early economic theories refer to it simply as labor, one of three factors of production, and consider it to be a fungible resource -- homogeneous and easily interchangeable. Other conceptions of labor dispense with these assumptions.

a. Law of increasing costs
b. Human capital
c. Price theory
d. General equilibrium

10. In general _____ refers to any non-human asset made by humans and then used in production. Often, it refers to economic capital in some ambiguous combination of infrastructural capital and natural capital. As these are combined in process-specific and firm-specific ways that neoclassical macroeconomics does not differentiate at its level of analysis, it is common to refer only to physical vs. human capital and seek so-called 'balanced growth' that develops both in tandem

Such analyses, however, fails to make distinctions considered critical by many modern economists.

a. Linkage principle
b. Factor cost
c. Net domestic product
d. Physical capital

Chapter 12. Technological Progress and Growth

1. In economics, the _____ functional form of production functions is widely used to represent the relationship of an output to inputs. It was proposed by Knut Wicksell (1851-1926), and tested against statistical evidence by Charles Cobb and Paul Douglas in 1900-1928.

For production, the function is

$$Y = AL^{\alpha}K^{\beta},$$

where:

- Y = total production (the monetary value of all goods produced in a year)
- L = labor input
- K = capital input
- A = total factor productivity
- α and β are the output elasticities of labor and capital, respectively. These values are constants determined by available technology.

Output elasticity measures the responsiveness of output to a change in levels of either labor or capital used in production, ceteris paribus. For example if α = 0.15, a 1% increase in labor would lead to approximately a 0.15% increase in output.

a. Cobb-Douglas
b. Demand-pull theory
c. Social savings
d. Growth accounting

2. In economics, _____ is the total supply of goods and services produced by a national economy during a specific time period. It is the total amount of goods and services in the economy available at all possible price levels.
a. Aggregation problem
b. Aggregate expenditure
c. Aggregate supply
d. Aggregate demand

3. Economics:

- _____ ,the desire to own something and the ability to pay for it
- _____ curve,a graphic representation of a _____ schedule
- _____ deposit, the money in checking accounts
- _____ pull theory,the theory that inflation occurs when _____ for goods and services exceeds existing supplies
- _____ schedule,a table that lists the quantity of a good a person will buy it each different price
- _____ side economics,the school of economics at believes government spending and tax cuts open economy by raising _____

a. McKesson ' Robbins scandal
b. Demand
c. Production
d. Variability

Chapter 12. Technological Progress and Growth

4. In microeconomics, _____ is quite simply the conversion of inputs into outputs. It is an economic process that uses resources to create a good or service that is suitable for exchange. This can include manufacturing, storing, shipping, and packaging.
   a. MET
   b. Red Guards
   c. Production
   d. Solved

5. In economics, a _____ is a function that specifies the output of a firm, an industry, or an entire economy for all combinations of inputs. A meta-_____ compares the practice of the existing entities converting inputs X into output y to determine the most efficient practice _____ of the existing entities, whether the most efficient feasible practice production or the most efficient actual practice production. In either case, the maximum output of a technologically-determined production process is a mathematical function of input factors of production.
   a. Post-Fordism
   b. Constant elasticity of substitution
   c. Short-run
   d. Production function

6. _____ is an economic model based on price, utility and quantity in a market. It predicts that in a competitive market, price will function to equalize the quantity demanded by consumers, and the quantity supplied by producers, resulting in an economic equilibrium of price and quantity. The model incorporates other factors changing equilibrium as a shift of demand and/or supply.
   a. Deferred gratification
   b. Joint demand
   c. Rational addiction
   d. Supply and demand

7. In financial accounting, the _____ is one of the accounts in shareholders' equity. Sole proprietorships have a single _____ in the owner's equity. Partnerships maintain a _____ for each of the partners.
   a. Current account
   b. Compensation of employees
   c. Net national product
   d. Capital account

8. In algebra, a _____ is a function depending on n that associates a scalar, det(A), to an n×n square matrix A. The fundamental geometric meaning of a _____ is a scale factor for measure when A is regarded as a linear transformation. _____s are important both in calculus, where they enter the substitution rule for several variables, and in multilinear algebra.

For a fixed nonnegative integer n, there is a unique _____ function for the n×n matrices over any commutative ring R. In particular, this function exists when R is the field of real or complex numbers.

   a. Determinant
   b. 1921 recession
   c. 130-30 fund
   d. 100-year flood

9. A _____ is a set of exclusive rights granted by a state to an inventor or his assignee for a limited period of time in exchange for a disclosure of an invention.

The procedure for granting _____s, the requirements placed on the _____ee and the extent of the exclusive rights vary widely between countries according to national laws and international agreements. Typically, however, a _____ application must include one or more claims defining the invention which must be new, inventive, and useful or industrially applicable.

a. Long service leave
b. Bona fide occupational qualification
c. Bank regulation
d. Patent

10. In economics, _____ describes a situation where a decision-maker's preferences change over time, such that what is preferred at one point in time is inconsistent with what is preferred at another point in time. It is often easiest to think about preferences over time in this context by thinking of decision-makers as being made up of many different 'selves', with each self representing the decision-maker at a different point in time. So, for example, there is my today self, my tomorrow self, my next Tuesday self, my year from now self, etc.

a. Bondareva-Shapley theorem
b. Graph continuous
c. Cheap talk
d. Dynamic inconsistency

11. In economics, accounting and Marxian economics, _____ is often equated with investment of profit income, especially in real capital goods. The concentration and centralisation of capital are two of the results of such accumulation

But _____ can refer variously to

- working and consuming less than earned
- relying on the effects of compound interest to increase initial capital
- real investment in tangible means of production.
- financial investment in assets represented on paper.
- investment in non-productive physical assets such as residential real estate that appreciate in value.
- consuming less than produced by productive assets like farm land--saving or accumulating the residual
- 'human _____,' i.e., new education and training increasing the skills of the labour force.

Non-financial and financial _____ is usually needed for economic growth, since additional production usually requires additional funds to enlarge the scale of production. Smarter and more productive organization of production can also increase production without increased capital.

a. Capital accumulation
b. Marxian economics
c. Productive force
d. Cultural Marxism

12. _____ is a type of private equity investment, most often a minority investment, in relatively mature companies that are looking for capital to expand or restructure operations, enter new markets or finance a significant acquisition without a change of control of the business.

Companies that seek _____, will often do so in order to finance a transformational event in their lifecycle. These companies are likely to be more mature than venture capital funded companies, able to generate revenue and operating profits but unable to generate sufficient cash to fund major expansions, acquisitions or other investments.

a. Club deal
b. Startup company
c. Seed money
d. Growth capital

Chapter 12. Technological Progress and Growth

13. The _____ or gross domestic income (GDI), a basic measure of an economy's economic performance, is the market value of all final goods and services produced within the borders of a nation in a year. _____ can be defined in three ways, all of which are conceptually identical. First, it is equal to the total expenditures for all final goods and services produced within the country in a stipulated period of time (usually a 365-day year.)
   a. Countercyclical
   b. Monopolistic competition
   c. Market structure
   d. Gross domestic product

14. A _____ is the exclusive authority to determine how a resource is used, whether that resource is owned by government or by individuals. All economic goods have a _____s attribute. This attribute has three broad components

   1. The right to use the good
   2. The right to earn income from the good
   3. The right to transfer the good to others

The concept of _____s as used by economists and legal scholars are related but distinct. The distinction is largely seen in the economists' focus on the ability of an individual or collective to control the use of the good.

   a. Holder in due course
   b. Post-sale restraint
   c. High-reeve
   d. Property right

15. An _____, in economics, is the amount by which the real Gross domestic product exceeds potential GDP. The real GDP is also known as GDP 'adjusted for inflation', 'constant prices' GDP or 'constant dollar' GDP, because it measures the aggregate output in a country's income accounts in a given year, expressed in base-year prices. On the other hand, the potential GDP is the quantity of real GDP when a country's economy is at full-employment.
   a. ACEA agreement
   b. AD-IA Model
   c. ACCRA Cost of Living Index
   d. Inflationary gap

16. The phrase _____, according to the Organization for Economic Co-operation and Development, refers to 'creative work undertaken on a systematic basis in order to increase the stock of knowledge, including knowledge of man, culture and society, and the use of this stock of knowledge to devise new applications [sic]'

New product design and development is more than often a crucial factor in the survival of a company. In an industry that is fast changing, firms must continually revise their design and range of products. This is necessary due to continuous technology change and development as well as other competitors and the changing preference of customers.

   a. 1921 recession
   b. Research and development
   c. 100-year flood
   d. 130-30 fund

17. _____ is a common concept in economics, and gives rise to derived concepts such as consumer debt. Generally _____ is defined by opposition to production. But the precise definition can vary because different schools of economists define production quite differently.
   a. Cash or share options
   b. Federal Reserve Bank Notes
   c. Consumption
   d. Foreclosure data providers

18. The _____ was an evolution of developed countries from an industrial/manufacturing-based wealth producing economy into a service sector asset based economy, brought about by globalization and currency manipulation by governments and their central banks. Some analysts claimed that this change in the economic structure of the United States had created a state of permanent steady growth, low unemployment, and immunity to boom and bust macroeconomic cycles. They believed that the change rendered obsolete many business practices.
   a. 100-year flood
   b. 130-30 fund
   c. New Economy
   d. 1921 recession

19. _____ in economics refers to metrics and measures of output from production processes, per unit of input. Labor _____, for example, is typically measured as a ratio of output per labor-hour, an input. _____ may be conceived of as a metrics of the technical or engineering efficiency of production.
   a. Piece work
   b. Production-possibility frontier
   c. Productivity
   d. Fordism

20. The _____ is a number describing empirical productivity growth in an economy from year to year and decade to decade. Robert Solow defined rising productivity as rising output with constant capital and labor input. It is a 'residual' because it is the part of growth that cannot be explained through capital accumulation.
   a. Quantity theory
   b. Solow residual
   c. Factor shares
   d. Secular basis

21. In economics, _____ (TFP) is a variable which accounts for effects in total output not caused by inputs. For example, a year with unusually good weather will tend to have higher output, because bad weather hinders agricultural output. A variable like weather does not directly relate to unit inputs, so weather is considered a _____ variable.
   a. Human rights
   b. Flow to Equity-Approach
   c. 35-hour working week
   d. Total-factor productivity

Chapter 13. Technological Progress, Wages, and Unemployment

1. In economics, the _____ is a historical inverse relation between the rate of unemployment and the rate of inflation in an economy. Stated simply, the lower the unemployment in an economy, the higher the rate of increase in nominal wages in the economy. Rate of Change of Wages against Unemployment, United Kingdom 1913-1948 from Phillips (1958)

William Phillips, a New Zealand born economist, wrote a paper in 1958 titled The Relationship between Unemployment and the Rate of Change of Money Wages in the United Kingdom 1861-1957, which was published in the quarterly journal Economica.

   a. Lorenz curve
   b. Cost curve
   c. Demand curve
   d. Phillips curve

2. _____ is a form of government in which scientists and technical experts are in administrative or decision making control. The term came to mean government by technical decision making in 1932.

There were a variety of Technocratic groups and organisations in a number of countries with a number of scientists, writers and others connected to ideas of thermoeconomics, bioeconomics and non-market economics.

   a. J26
   b. Variability
   c. Boulton ' Watt
   d. Technocracy

3. In economics, _____ is the total demand for final goods and services in the economy (Y) at a given time and price level. It is the amount of goods and services in the economy that will be purchased at all possible price levels. This is the demand for the gross domestic product of a country when inventory levels are static.
   a. Aggregation problem
   b. Aggregate demand
   c. Aggregate supply
   d. Aggregate expenditure

4. In economics, _____ is the total supply of goods and services produced by a national economy during a specific time period. It is the total amount of goods and services in the economy available at all possible price levels.
   a. Aggregate demand
   b. Aggregate expenditure
   c. Aggregation problem
   d. Aggregate supply

5. _____ in economics refers to metrics and measures of output from production processes, per unit of input. Labor _____, for example, is typically measured as a ratio of output per labor-hour, an input. _____ may be conceived of as a metrics of the technical or engineering efficiency of production.
   a. Productivity
   b. Production-possibility frontier
   c. Piece work
   d. Fordism

Chapter 13. Technological Progress, Wages, and Unemployment

6. Economics:

    - _____,the desire to own something and the ability to pay for it
    - _____ curve,a graphic representation of a _____ schedule
    - _____ deposit, the money in checking accounts
    - _____ pull theory,the theory that inflation occurs when _____ for goods and services exceeds existing supplies
    - _____ schedule,a table that lists the quantity of a good a person will buy it each different price
    - _____ side economics,the school of economics at believes government spending and tax cuts open economy by raising _____

    a. Demand
    c. Variability
    b. Production
    d. McKesson ' Robbins scandal

7. _____ is an economic model based on price, utility and quantity in a market. It predicts that in a competitive market, price will function to equalize the quantity demanded by consumers, and the quantity supplied by producers, resulting in an economic equilibrium of price and quantity. The model incorporates other factors changing equilibrium as a shift of demand and/or supply.
    a. Joint demand
    c. Deferred gratification
    b. Rational addiction
    d. Supply and demand

8. The term _____s refers to wages that have been adjusted for inflation. This term is used in contrast to nominal wages or unadjusted wages.

The use of adjusted figures is in undertaking some form of economic analysis.

    a. Profit sharing
    c. Living wage
    b. Real wage
    d. Federal Wage System

9. The _____ is a concept of economic activity developed in particular by Milton Friedman and Edmund Phelps in the 1960s, both recipients of the Nobel prize in economics. In both cases, the development of the concept is cited as a main motivation behind the prize. It represents the hypothetical unemployment rate consistent with aggregate production being at the 'long-run' level.
    a. Romer Model
    c. Robertson lag
    b. Natural rate of unemployment
    d. Real Business Cycle Theory

10. The _____ was an evolution of developed countries from an industrial/manufacturing-based wealth producing economy into a service sector asset based economy, brought about by globalization and currency manipulation by governments and their central banks. Some analysts claimed that this change in the economic structure of the United States had created a state of permanent steady growth, low unemployment, and immunity to boom and bust macroeconomic cycles. They believed that the change rendered obsolete many business practices.
    a. 1921 recession
    c. 100-year flood
    b. 130-30 fund
    d. New Economy

Chapter 13. Technological Progress, Wages, and Unemployment

11. The _____ or gross domestic income (GDI), a basic measure of an economy's economic performance, is the market value of all final goods and services produced within the borders of a nation in a year. _____ can be defined in three ways, all of which are conceptually identical. First, it is equal to the total expenditures for all final goods and services produced within the country in a stipulated period of time (usually a 365-day year.)
   a. Monopolistic competition
   b. Countercyclical
   c. Market structure
   d. Gross domestic product

12. The notion of _____ is found in the writings of Mikhail Bakunin, Friedrich Nietzsche, and in Werner Sombart's Krieg und Kapitalismus (War and Capitalism) (1913, p. 207), where he wrote: 'again out of destruction a new spirit of creativity arises'. In Capitalism, Socialism and Democracy, the Austrian economist Joseph Schumpeter popularized and used the term to describe the process of transformation that accompanies radical innovation.
   a. 1921 recession
   b. 130-30 fund
   c. Creative destruction
   d. 100-year flood

13. _____ of an economy refers to a long-term widespread change of the fundamental structure, rather than microscale or short-term output and employment. For example, a subsistence economy is transformed into a manufacturing economy, or a regulated mixed economy is liberalized. A current _____ in the world economy is globalization.
   a. Structural change
   b. Fiscal adjustment
   c. Dishoarding
   d. Robertson lag

14. In mathematics, an _____ is a statement about the relative size or order of two objects, or about whether they are the same or not

   - The notation a < b means that a is less than b.
   - The notation a > b means that a is greater than b.
   - The notation a ≠ b means that a is not equal to b, but does not say that one is greater than the other or even that they can be compared in size.

   In each statement above, a is not equal to b. These relations are known as strict inequalities. The notation a < b may also be read as 'a is strictly less than b'.

   a. Inequality
   b. AD-IA Model
   c. ACEA agreement
   d. ACCRA Cost of Living Index

15. The _____ is an economic and political union of 27 member states, located primarily in Europe. It was established by the Treaty of Maastricht on 1 November 1993, upon the foundations of the pre-existing European Economic Community. With a population of almost 500 million, the _____ generates an estimated 30% share (US$18.4 trillion in 2008) of the nominal gross world product.
   a. European Court of Justice
   b. ACCRA Cost of Living Index
   c. ACEA agreement
   d. European Union

16. _____ is a term coined in the 1980s to describe a European economic pattern of high unemployment and slow job creation in spite of overall economic growth. This was in contrast to what the United States experienced in the same period when economic expansion was accompanied by high job growth. Later, the term tended to be used more broadly to refer to overall economic stagnation.

a. Agency shop
b. Indivisibility of labor
c. Entry-level job
d. Eurosclerosis

Chapter 14. Expectations: The Basic Tools

1. In finance and economics _____ or nominal rate of interest refers to the rate of interest before adjustment for inflation (in contrast with the real interest rate); or, for interest rates 'as stated' without adjustment for the full effect of compounding (also referred to as the nominal annual rate.) An interest rate is called nominal if the frequency of compounding (e.g. a month) is not identical to the basic time unit (normally a year.)

The real interest rate includes compensation for the lender's lost value due to inflation, whereas the _____ excludes inflation.

   a. London Interbank Offered Rate
   b. Nominal interest rate
   c. Risk-free interest rate
   d. Fixed interest

2. The '_____' is approximately the nominal interest rate minus the inflation rate Since the inflation rate over the course of a loan is not known initially, volatility in inflation represents a risk to both the lender and the borrower.

In economics and finance, an individual who lends money for repayment at a later point in time expects to be compensated for the time value of money, or not having the use of that money while it is lent.

   a. Cost-push inflation
   b. Core inflation
   c. Reflation
   d. Real interest rate

3. _____ is a fee paid on borrowed assets. It is the price paid for the use of borrowed money , or, money earned by deposited funds . Assets that are sometimes lent with _____ include money, shares, consumer goods through hire purchase, major assets such as aircraft, and even entire factories in finance lease arrangements.
   a. Internal debt
   b. Interest
   c. Insolvency
   d. Asset protection

4. An _____ is the price a borrower pays for the use of money they do not own, for instance a small company might borrow from a bank to kick start their business, and the return a lender receives for deferring the use of funds, by lending it to the borrower. _____s are normally expressed as a percentage rate over the period of one year.

_____s targets are also a vital tool of monetary policy and are used to control variables like investment, inflation, and unemployment.

   a. Arrow-Debreu model
   b. Interest rate
   c. Enterprise value
   d. ACCRA Cost of Living Index

5. The _____ was a worldwide economic downturn starting in most places in 1929 and ending at different times in the 1930s or early 1940s for different countries. It was the largest and most important economic depression in the 20th century, and is used in the 21st century as an example of how far the world's economy can fall. The _____ originated in the United States; historians most often use as a starting date the stock market crash on October 29, 1929, known as Black Tuesday.
   a. Wall Street Crash of 1929
   b. British Empire Economic Conference
   c. Jarrow March
   d. Great Depression

Chapter 14. Expectations: The Basic Tools

6. The _____ was an evolution of developed countries from an industrial/manufacturing-based wealth producing economy into a service sector asset based economy, brought about by globalization and currency manipulation by governments and their central banks. Some analysts claimed that this change in the economic structure of the United States had created a state of permanent steady growth, low unemployment, and immunity to boom and bust macroeconomic cycles. They believed that the change rendered obsolete many business practices.

   a. 1921 recession
   b. 130-30 fund
   c. 100-year flood
   d. New Economy

7. _____ is the value on a given date of a future payment or series of future payments, discounted to reflect the time value of money and other factors such as investment risk. _____ calculations are widely used in business and economics to provide a means to compare cash flows at different times on a meaningful 'like to like' basis.

Money value fluctuates over time: $100 today are not worth $100 in five years.

   a. Tax shield
   b. Present value of costs
   c. Future value
   d. Present value

8. _____ is the a method of technical and economic research of the systems for purpose to optimize a parity between system's consumer functions or properties and expenses to achieve those functions or properties.

This methodology for continuous perfection of production, industrial technologies, organizational structures was developed by Juryj Sobolev in 1948 at the 'Perm telephone factory'

- 1948 Juryj Sobolev - the first success in application of a method analysis at the 'Perm telephone factory' .
- 1949 - the first application for the invention as result of use of the new method.

Today in economically developed countries practically each enterprise or the company use methodology of the kind of functional-cost analysis as a practice of the quality management, most full satisfying to principles of standards of series ISO 9000.

- Interest of consumer not in products itself, but the advantage which it will receive from its usage.
- The consumer aspires to reduce his expenses
- Functions needed by consumer can be executed in the various ways, and, hence, with various efficiency and expenses. Among possible alternatives of realization of functions exist such in which the parity of quality and the price is the optimal for the consumer.

The goal of _____ is achievement of the highest consumer satisfaction of production at simultaneous decrease in all kinds of industrial expenses Classical _____ has three English synonyms - Value Engineering, Value Management, Value Analysis.

   a. Monopoly wage
   b. Staple financing
   c. Willingness to pay
   d. Function cost analysis

Chapter 14. Expectations: The Basic Tools

9. Discounting is a financial mechanism in which a debtor obtains the right to delay payments to a creditor, for a defined period of time, in exchange for a charge or fee. Essentially, the party that owes money in the present purchases the right to delay the payment until some future date. The _____, or charge, is simply the difference between the original amount owed in the present and the amount that has to be paid in the future to settle the debt.
   a. Certified Risk Manager
   b. Reliability theory
   c. Reinsurance
   d. Discount

10. The _____ is an interest rate a central bank charges depository institutions that borrow reserves from it.

The term _____ has two meanings:

- the same as interest rate; the term 'discount' does not refer to the meaning of the word, but to the purpose of using the quantity, such as computations of present value, e.g. net present value or discounted cash flow

- the annual effective _____, which is the annual interest divided by the capital including that interest; this rate is lower than the interest rate; it corresponds to using the value after a year as the nominal value, and seeing the initial value as the nominal value minus a discount; it is used for Treasury Bills and similar financial instruments

The annual effective _____ is the annual interest divided by the capital including that interest, which is the interest rate divided by 100% plus the interest rate. It is the annual discount factor to be applied to the future cash flow, to find the discount, subtracted from a future value to find the value one year earlier.

For example, suppose there is a government bond that sells for $95 and pays $100 in a year's time.

   a. Johansen test
   b. Perpetuity
   c. Stochastic volatility
   d. Discount rate

11. A _____ is the transfer of wealth from one party (such as a person or company) to another. A _____ is usually made in exchange for the provision of goods, services or both, or to fulfill a legal obligation.

The simplest and oldest form of _____ is barter, the exchange of one good or service for another.

   a. Soft count
   b. Social gravity
   c. Going concern
   d. Payment

12. A _____, reserve bank, or monetary authority is the entity responsible for the monetary policy of a country or of a group of member states. It is a bank that can lend money to other banks in times of need. Its primary responsibility is to maintain the stability of the national currency and money supply, but more active duties include controlling subsidized-loan interest rates, and acting as a lender of last resort to the banking sector during times of financial crisis (private banks often being integral to the national financial system.)
   a. Central bank
   b. 100-year flood
   c. 1921 recession
   d. 130-30 fund

Chapter 14. Expectations: The Basic Tools

13. In finance, a _____ is a debt security, in which the authorized issuer owes the holders a debt and, depending on the terms of the _____, is obliged to pay interest (the coupon) and/or to repay the principal at a later date, termed maturity. A _____ is a formal contract to repay borrowed money with interest at fixed intervals.

Thus a _____ is like a loan: the issuer is the borrower (debtor), the holder is the lender (creditor), and the coupon is the interest.

a. Bond
b. Prize Bond
c. Zero-coupon
d. Callable

14. In economics, _____ is a rise in the general level of prices of goods and services in an economy over a period of time. When the general price level rises, each unit of currency buys fewer goods and services; consequently, _____ is also a decline in the real value of money--a loss of purchasing power in the medium of exchange which is also the monetary unit of account in the economy. A chief measure of general price-level _____ is the general _____ rate, which is the percentage change in a general price index (normally the Consumer Price Index) over time.

a. Energy economics
b. Economic
c. Opportunity cost
d. Inflation

15. In economics, the _____ is the proposition by Irving Fisher that the real interest rate is independent of monetary measures, especially the nominal interest rate. The Fisher equation is

$$r_r = r_n - \pi^e.$$

This means, the real interest rate (r_r) equals the nominal interest rate (r_n) minus expected rate of inflation (π^e.) Here all the rates are continuously compounded.

a. Marginal revenue productivity theory of wages
b. Core competency
c. Khazzoom-Brookes postulate
d. Fisher hypothesis

16. _____ was an American economist, statistician and public intellectual, and a recipient of the Nobel Memorial Prize in Economic Sciences. He is best known among scholars for his theoretical and empirical research, especially consumption analysis, monetary history and theory, and for his demonstration of the complexity of stabilization policy. A global public followed his restatement of a political philosophy that insisted on minimizing the role of government in favor of the private sector.

a. Adam Smith
b. Adolph Fischer
c. Adolf Hitler
d. Milton Friedman

Chapter 15. Financial Markets and Expectations

1. In finance, a _____ is a debt security, in which the authorized issuer owes the holders a debt and, depending on the terms of the _____, is obliged to pay interest (the coupon) and/or to repay the principal at a later date, termed maturity. A _____ is a formal contract to repay borrowed money with interest at fixed intervals.

Thus a _____ is like a loan: the issuer is the borrower (debtor), the holder is the lender (creditor), and the coupon is the interest.

   a. Bond
   b. Prize Bond
   c. Zero-coupon
   d. Callable

2. _____ is a life of security. It may also refer to the final payment date of a loan or other financial instrument, at which point all remaining interest and principal is due to be paid.

1, 3, 6 months _____ band can be calculated by using 30-day per month periods.

   a. Future-oriented
   b. Refinancing risk
   c. Future value
   d. Maturity

3. _____ is a fee paid on borrowed assets. It is the price paid for the use of borrowed money, or, money earned by deposited funds. Assets that are sometimes lent with _____ include money, shares, consumer goods through hire purchase, major assets such as aircraft, and even entire factories in finance lease arrangements.

   a. Asset protection
   b. Interest
   c. Internal debt
   d. Insolvency

4. An _____ is the price a borrower pays for the use of money they do not own, for instance a small company might borrow from a bank to kick start their business, and the return a lender receives for deferring the use of funds, by lending it to the borrower. _____s are normally expressed as a percentage rate over the period of one year.

_____s targets are also a vital tool of monetary policy and are used to control variables like investment, inflation, and unemployment.

   a. Enterprise value
   b. Arrow-Debreu model
   c. ACCRA Cost of Living Index
   d. Interest rate

5. _____ in economics and business is the result of an exchange and from that trade we assign a numerical monetary value to a good, service or asset. If Alice trades Bob 4 apples for an orange, the _____ of an orange is 4 apples. Inversely, the _____ of an apple is 1/4 oranges.

   a. Price book
   b. Price
   c. Price war
   d. Premium pricing

6. A _____ is a bond issued by a corporation. It is a bond that a corporation issues to raise money in order to expand its business. The term is usually applied to longer-term debt instruments, generally with a maturity date falling at least a year after their issue date.

   a. Bond valuation
   b. Dirty price
   c. Corporate bond
   d. Bond fund

Chapter 15. Financial Markets and Expectations

7. The _____, interest yield, income yield, flat yield or running yield is a financial term used in reference to bonds and other fixed-interest securities such as gilts. It is the ratio of the annual interest payment and the bond's current clean price:

$$\text{Current yield} = \frac{\text{Annual interest payment}}{\text{Clean price}}.$$

The _____ only therefore refers to the yield of the bond at the current moment. It does not reflect the total return over the life of the bond.

a. Stochastic volatility
b. Current yield
c. LIBOR market model
d. Mathematical finance

8. Discounting is a financial mechanism in which a debtor obtains the right to delay payments to a creditor, for a defined period of time, in exchange for a charge or fee. Essentially, the party that owes money in the present purchases the right to delay the payment until some future date. The _____, or charge, is simply the difference between the original amount owed in the present and the amount that has to be paid in the future to settle the debt.

a. Reliability theory
b. Discount
c. Certified Risk Manager
d. Reinsurance

9. _____ is the value of a coin, stamp or paper money, as printed on the coin, stamp or bill itself by the minting authority. While the _____ usually refers to the true value of the coin, stamp or bill in question (as with circulation coins) it can sometimes be largely symbolic, as is often the case with bullion coins. For example, a one troy ounce (31 g) American Gold Eagle bullion coin was worth and sold for about $670 USD during 2006 market prices (as of July 17, 2006) and yet has a _____ of only $50 USD.

a. 100-year flood
b. Face value
c. 130-30 fund
d. Money Tracker

10. A _____ is the minimum difference a person requires to be willing to take an uncertain bet, between the expected value of the bet and the certain value that he is indifferent to.

The certainty equivalent is the guaranteed payoff at which a person is 'indifferent' between accepting the guaranteed payoff and a higher but uncertain payoff. (It is the amount of the higher payout minus the _____.)

a. Linear model
b. Ruin theory
c. Workers compensation
d. Risk premium

11. A United States Treasury security is a government debt issued by the United States Department of the Treasury through the Bureau of the Public Debt. Treasury securities are the debt financing instruments of the United States Federal government, and they are often referred to simply as Treasuries. There are four types of marketable treasury securities: _____, Treasury notes, Treasury bonds, and Treasury Inflation Protected Securities (TIPS.)

a. Debt to Assets
b. Lawcards
c. Labour battalions
d. Treasury bills

Chapter 15. Financial Markets and Expectations

12. A _____ is the transfer of wealth from one party (such as a person or company) to another. A _____ is usually made in exchange for the provision of goods, services or both, or to fulfill a legal obligation.

The simplest and oldest form of _____ is barter, the exchange of one good or service for another.

a. Going concern
b. Soft count
c. Social gravity
d. Payment

13. _____ is the a method of technical and economic research of the systems for purpose to optimize a parity between system's consumer functions or properties and expenses to achieve those functions or properties.

This methodology for continuous perfection of production, industrial technologies, organizational structures was developed by Juryj Sobolev in 1948 at the 'Perm telephone factory'

- 1948 Juryj Sobolev - the first success in application of a method analysis at the 'Perm telephone factory' .
- 1949 - the first application for the invention as result of use of the new method.

Today in economically developed countries practically each enterprise or the company use methodology of the kind of functional-cost analysis as a practice of the quality management, most full satisfying to principles of standards of series ISO 9000.

- Interest of consumer not in products itself, but the advantage which it will receive from its usage.
- The consumer aspires to reduce his expenses
- Functions needed by consumer can be executed in the various ways, and, hence, with various efficiency and expenses. Among possible alternatives of realization of functions exist such in which the parity of quality and the price is the optimal for the consumer.

The goal of _____ is achievement of the highest consumer satisfaction of production at simultaneous decrease in all kinds of industrial expenses Classical _____ has three English synonyms - Value Engineering, Value Management, Value Analysis.

a. Function cost analysis
b. Willingness to pay
c. Staple financing
d. Monopoly wage

14. In economics and finance, _____ is the practice of taking advantage of a price differential between two or more markets: striking a combination of matching deals that capitalize upon the imbalance, the profit being the difference between the market prices. When used by academics, an _____ is a transaction that involves no negative cash flow at any probabilistic or temporal state and a positive cash flow in at least one state; in simple terms, a risk-free profit. A person who engages in _____ is called an arbitrageur--such as a bank or brokerage firm.

a. Alternext
b. Options Price Reporting Authority
c. Arbitrage
d. Electronic trading

15. _____ is the value on a given date of a future payment or series of future payments, discounted to reflect the time value of money and other factors such as investment risk. _____ calculations are widely used in business and economics to provide a means to compare cash flows at different times on a meaningful 'like to like' basis.

Money value fluctuates over time: $100 today are not worth $100 in five years.

   a. Tax shield
   b. Future value
   c. Present value of costs
   d. Present value

16. The _____ or redemption yield is the yield promised to the bondholder on the assumption that the bond or other fixed-interest security such as gilts will be held to maturity, that all coupon and principal payments will be made and coupon payments are reinvested at the bond's promised yield at the same rate as the original principal invested. It is a measure of the return of the bond. This technique in theory allows investors to calculate the fair value of different financial instruments.
   a. Yield to maturity
   b. Bond duration closed-form formula
   c. Fixed income analysis
   d. Closed-form formula

17. _____s is the social science that studies the production, distribution, and consumption of goods and services. The term _____s comes from the Ancient Greek οἰκονομία from οἶκος (oikos, 'house') + νόμος (nomos, 'custom' or 'law'), hence 'rules of the house(hold)'. Current _____ models developed out of the broader field of political economy in the late 19th century, owing to a desire to use an empirical approach more akin to the physical sciences.
   a. Inflation
   b. Energy economics
   c. Economic
   d. Opportunity cost

18. In economics, _____ is inflation that is very high or 'out of control', a condition in which prices increase rapidly as a currency loses its value. Definitions used by the media vary from a cumulative inflation rate over three years approaching 100% to 'inflation exceeding 50% a month.' In informal usage the term is often applied to much lower rates. As a rule of thumb, normal inflation is reported per year, but _____ is often reported for much shorter intervals, often per month.
   a. Hyperinflation
   b. 130-30 fund
   c. 100-year flood
   d. 1921 recession

19. _____ is that which is owed; usually referencing assets owed, but the term can also cover moral obligations and other interactions not requiring money. In the case of assets, _____ is a means of using future purchasing power in the present before a summation has been earned. Some companies and corporations use _____ as a part of their overall corporate finance strategy.
   a. Debenture
   b. Collateral Management
   c. Hard money loan
   d. Debt

20. _____s are payments made by a corporation to its shareholders. It is the portion of corporate profits paid out to stockholders. When a corporation earns a profit or surplus, that money can be put to two uses: it can either be re-invested in the business (called retained earnings), or it can be paid to the shareholders as a _____.
   a. Dividend puzzle
   b. Dividend cover
   c. Dividend yield
   d. Dividend

21. _____ is the concept or idea of fairness in economics, particularly as to taxation or welfare economics.

In welfare economics, _____ may be distinguished from economic efficiency in overall evaluation of social welfare. Although '_____' has broader uses, it may be posed as a counterpart to economic inequality in yielding a 'good' distribution of welfare.

Chapter 15. Financial Markets and Expectations

a. ACCRA Cost of Living Index
b. AD-IA Model
c. ACEA agreement
d. Equity

22. A _____ is a method of measuring a section of the stock market. Many indices are cited by news or financial services firms and are used to benchmark the performance of portfolios such as mutual funds.

Stock market indices may be classed in many ways.

a. Stock market index
b. Lock up period
c. Scrip issue
d. Stock market bubble

23. _____ is a concept with somewhat disparate meanings in several fields. It also has a common meaning which has a loose connection with some of those more definite meanings.

Casually, it is typically used to denote a lack of order, or purpose, or cause.

a. Randomness
b. 130-30 fund
c. 100-year flood
d. 1921 recession

24. A _____, sometimes denoted _____, is a mathematical formalization of a trajectory that consists of taking successive random steps. The results of _____ analysis have been applied to computer science, physics, ecology, economics, and a number of other fields as a fundamental model for random processes in time. For example, the path traced by a molecule as it travels in a liquid or a gas, the search path of a foraging animal, the price of a fluctuating stock and the financial status of a gambler can all be modeled as _____s.

a. 100-year flood
b. 130-30 fund
c. 1921 recession
d. Random walk

25. A _____ is a public market for the trading of company stock and derivatives at an agreed price; these are securities listed on a stock exchange as well as those only traded privately.

The size of the world _____ was estimated at about $36.6 trillion US at the beginning of October 2008 . The total world derivatives market has been estimated at about $791 trillion face or nominal value, 11 times the size of the entire world economy.

a. Adolf Hitler
b. Adam Smith
c. Adolph Fischer
d. Stock market

26. _____ is a broad label that refers to any individuals or households that use goods and services generated within the economy. The concept of a _____ is used in different contexts, so that the usage and significance of the term may vary.

Typically when business people and economists talk of _____s they are talking about person as _____, an aggregated commodity item with little individuality other than that expressed in the buy/not-buy decision.

Chapter 15. Financial Markets and Expectations

a. 130-30 fund
b. Consumer
c. 100-year flood
d. 1921 recession

27. _____ or consumer demand or consumption is also known as personal consumption expenditure. It is the largest part of aggregate demand or effective demand at the macroeconomic level. There are two variants of consumption in the aggregate demand model, including induced consumption and autonomous consumption.

a. Dishoarding
b. Potential output
c. Consumer spending
d. Complex multiplier

28. _____ is a common concept in economics, and gives rise to derived concepts such as consumer debt. Generally _____ is defined by opposition to production. But the precise definition can vary because different schools of economists define production quite differently.

a. Consumption
b. Cash or share options
c. Federal Reserve Bank Notes
d. Foreclosure data providers

29. _____ is an American economist and was the Chairman of the Federal Reserve of the United States from 1987 to 2006. He currently works as a private advisor and providing consulting for firms through his company, Greenspan Associates LLC.

First appointed Federal Reserve chairman by President Ronald Reagan in August 1987, he was reappointed at successive four-year intervals until retiring on January 31, 2006 after the second-longest tenure in the position.

a. Adam Smith
b. Adolf Hitler
c. Adolph Fischer
d. Alan Greenspan

30. In economics, _____ behavior is in between risk aversion and risk seeking. If offered either â‚¬50 or a 50% chance of â‚¬100, a risk averse person will take the â‚¬50, a risk seeking person will take the 50% chance of â‚¬100, and a _____ person would have no preference between the two options.

In finance, when pricing an asset, a common technique is to figure out the probability of a future cash flow, then to discount that cash flow at the risk free rate.

a. Risk neutral
b. Transaction risk
c. Currency risk
d. Taleb distribution

Chapter 16. Expectations, Consumption, and Investment

1. _____ is a common concept in economics, and gives rise to derived concepts such as consumer debt. Generally _____ is defined by opposition to production. But the precise definition can vary because different schools of economists define production quite differently.
   - a. Consumption
   - b. Foreclosure data providers
   - c. Federal Reserve Bank Notes
   - d. Cash or share options

2. _____ was an American economist, statistician and public intellectual, and a recipient of the Nobel Memorial Prize in Economic Sciences. He is best known among scholars for his theoretical and empirical research, especially consumption analysis, monetary history and theory, and for his demonstration of the complexity of stabilization policy. A global public followed his restatement of a political philosophy that insisted on minimizing the role of government in favor of the private sector.
   - a. Adolph Fischer
   - b. Adolf Hitler
   - c. Adam Smith
   - d. Milton Friedman

3. The _____ is the worlde;s longest running household panel survey. The PSID is a longitudinal panel survey of United States families that measures economic, social, and health factors over the life course and across generations. Data have been collected from the same families and their descendants since 1968.
   - a. Symbolic capital
   - b. Deskilling
   - c. Gender Parity Index
   - d. Panel Study of Income Dynamics

4. In statistics and econometrics, the term _____ refers to two-dimensional data. In marketing, _____ refers to data collected at the point-of-sale (also called scanner data.)

   Data is broadly classified according to the number of dimensions.

   - a. Dynamic factor
   - b. Delta method
   - c. Hausman test
   - d. Panel data

5. _____ is a term used in business accounts, tax assessments and national accounts for depreciation of fixed assets. CFC is used in preference to 'depreciation' to emphasize that fixed capital is used up in the process of generating new output; CFC may include other costs incurred in using fixed assets beyond actual depreciation charges. Normally the term applies only to producing enterprises, but sometimes it applies also to real estate assets.
   - a. Firm-specific infrastructure
   - b. Modigliani-Miller theorem
   - c. Capital goods
   - d. Consumption of fixed capital

6. _____ is a broad label that refers to any individuals or households that use goods and services generated within the economy. The concept of a _____ is used in different contexts, so that the usage and significance of the term may vary.

   Typically when business people and economists talk of _____s they are talking about person as _____, an aggregated commodity item with little individuality other than that expressed in the buy/not-buy decision.

   - a. 1921 recession
   - b. 100-year flood
   - c. 130-30 fund
   - d. Consumer

Chapter 16. Expectations, Consumption, and Investment

7. _____ is the point where a person stops employment completely. A person may also semi-retire and keep some sort of _____ job, out of choice rather than necessity. This usually happens upon reaching a determined age, when physical conditions don't allow the person to work any more (by illness or accident), or even for personal choice (usually in the presence of an adequate pension or personal savings.)

   a. 100-year flood
   b. Retirement
   c. Layoff
   d. Termination of employment

8. The _____ is a statistical survey conducted by the Demographic Statistical Methods Division of the United States Census Bureau. The main objective of the SIPP is to provide accurate and comprehensive information about the income of American individuals and households and the participation of these people in income transfer programs.

   SIPP data allow the government to evaluate the effectiveness of Federal, state, and local programs.

   a. 130-30 fund
   b. 100-year flood
   c. 1921 recession
   d. Survey of Income and Program Participation

9. _____ is a term used in accounting, economics and finance to spread the cost of an asset over the span of several years.

   In simple words we can say that _____ is the reduction in the value of an asset due to usage, passage of time, wear and tear, technological outdating or obsolescence, depletion, inadequacy, rot, rust, decay or other such factors.

   In accounting, _____ is a term used to describe any method of attributing the historical or purchase cost of an asset across its useful life, roughly corresponding to normal wear and tear.

   a. Historical cost
   b. Depreciation
   c. Net income per employee
   d. Salvage value

10. _____ is the value on a given date of a future payment or series of future payments, discounted to reflect the time value of money and other factors such as investment risk. _____ calculations are widely used in business and economics to provide a means to compare cash flows at different times on a meaningful 'like to like' basis.

    Money value fluctuates over time: $100 today are not worth $100 in five years.

    a. Present value of costs
    b. Future value
    c. Tax shield
    d. Present value

11. _____ is the a method of technical and economic research of the systems for purpose to optimize a parity between system's consumer functions or properties and expenses to achieve those functions or properties.

Chapter 16. Expectations, Consumption, and Investment

This methodology for continuous perfection of production, industrial technologies, organizational structures was developed by Juryj Sobolev in 1948 at the 'Perm telephone factory'

- 1948 Juryj Sobolev - the first success in application of a method analysis at the 'Perm telephone factory' .
- 1949 - the first application for the invention as result of use of the new method.

Today in economically developed countries practically each enterprise or the company use methodology of the kind of functional-cost analysis as a practice of the quality management, most full satisfying to principles of standards of series ISO 9000.

- Interest of consumer not in products itself, but the advantage which it will receive from its usage.
- The consumer aspires to reduce his expenses
- Functions needed by consumer can be executed in the various ways, and, hence, with various efficiency and expenses. Among possible alternatives of realization of functions exist such in which the parity of quality and the price is the optimal for the consumer.

The goal of _____ is achievement of the highest consumer satisfaction of production at simultaneous decrease in all kinds of industrial expenses Classical _____ has three English synonyms - Value Engineering, Value Management, Value Analysis.

a. Willingness to pay
c. Monopoly wage
b. Staple financing
d. Function cost analysis

12. _____ are made by investors and investment managers.

Investors commonly perform investment analysis by making use of fundamental analysis, technical analysis and gut feel.

_____ are often supported by decision tools.

a. Arbitrage betting
c. Investment strategy
b. Inventory investment
d. Investment decisions

13. _____ is a fee paid on borrowed assets. It is the price paid for the use of borrowed money , or, money earned by deposited funds . Assets that are sometimes lent with _____ include money, shares, consumer goods through hire purchase, major assets such as aircraft, and even entire factories in finance lease arrangements.

a. Internal debt
c. Insolvency
b. Interest
d. Asset protection

14. An _____ is the price a borrower pays for the use of money they do not own, for instance a small company might borrow from a bank to kick start their business, and the return a lender receives for deferring the use of funds, by lending it to the borrower. _____s are normally expressed as a percentage rate over the period of one year.

_____s targets are also a vital tool of monetary policy and are used to control variables like investment, inflation, and unemployment.

a. Arrow-Debreu model
c. Enterprise value
b. ACCRA Cost of Living Index
d. Interest rate

15. A _____ is a public market for the trading of company stock and derivatives at an agreed price; these are securities listed on a stock exchange as well as those only traded privately.

The size of the world _____ was estimated at about $36.6 trillion US at the beginning of October 2008 . The total world derivatives market has been estimated at about $791 trillion face or nominal value, 11 times the size of the entire world economy.

a. Adolf Hitler
c. Adam Smith
b. Adolph Fischer
d. Stock market

16. _____s is the social science that studies the production, distribution, and consumption of goods and services. The term _____s comes from the Ancient Greek oá¼°κονομῖα from oá¼¶κος (oikos, 'house') + vÏŒμος (nomos, 'custom' or 'law'), hence 'rules of the house(hold)'. Current _____ models developed out of the broader field of political economy in the late 19th century, owing to a desire to use an empirical approach more akin to the physical sciences.

a. Opportunity cost
c. Inflation
b. Energy economics
d. Economic

17. In financial accounting, the _____ is one of the accounts in shareholders' equity. Sole proprietorships have a single _____ in the owner's equity. Partnerships maintain a _____ for each of the partners.

a. Current account
c. Net national product
b. Compensation of employees
d. Capital account

18. The _____ is an expected return that the provider of capital plans to earn on their investment.

Capital (money) used for funding a business should earn returns for the capital providers who risk their capital. For an investment to be worthwhile, the expected return on capital must be greater than the _____.

a. Capital expenditure
c. Capital intensive
b. Modigliani-Miller theorem
d. Cost of Capital

Chapter 16. Expectations, Consumption, and Investment

19. _____ refers to the movement of cash into or out of a business or financial product. It is usually measured during a specified, finite period of time. Measurement of _____ can be used

- to determine a project's rate of return or value. The time of _____s into and out of projects are used as inputs in financial models such as internal rate of return, and net present value.
- to determine problems with a business's liquidity. Being profitable does not necessarily mean being liquid. A company can fail because of a shortage of cash, even while profitable.
- as an alternate measure of a business's profits when it is believed that accrual accounting concepts do not represent economic realities. For example, a company may be notionally profitable but generating little operational cash (as may be the case for a company that barters its products rather than selling for cash.) In such a case, the company may be deriving additional operating cash by issuing shares evaluating default risk, re-investment requirements, etc.

_____ is a generic term used differently depending on the context. It may be defined by users for their own purposes.

a. Second lien loan
b. Cash flow
c. Restricted stock
d. Strip financing

Chapter 17. Expectations, Output, and Policy

1. _____ is a common concept in economics, and gives rise to derived concepts such as consumer debt. Generally _____ is defined by opposition to production. But the precise definition can vary because different schools of economists define production quite differently.
   - a. Consumption
   - b. Federal Reserve Bank Notes
   - c. Cash or share options
   - d. Foreclosure data providers

2. In economics, _____ is the total demand for final goods and services in the economy (Y) at a given time and price level. It is the amount of goods and services in the economy that will be purchased at all possible price levels. This is the demand for the gross domestic product of a country when inventory levels are static.
   - a. Aggregate supply
   - b. Aggregate demand
   - c. Aggregation problem
   - d. Aggregate expenditure

3. Economics:
   - _____, the desire to own something and the ability to pay for it
   - _____ curve, a graphic representation of a _____ schedule
   - _____ deposit, the money in checking accounts
   - _____ pull theory, the theory that inflation occurs when _____ for goods and services exceeds existing supplies
   - _____ schedule, a table that lists the quantity of a good a person will buy it each different price
   - _____ side economics, the school of economics at believes government spending and tax cuts open economy by raising _____

   - a. Variability
   - b. Demand
   - c. McKesson ' Robbins scandal
   - d. Production

4. _____ are made by investors and investment managers.

   Investors commonly perform investment analysis by making use of fundamental analysis, technical analysis and gut feel.

   _____ are often supported by decision tools.

   - a. Arbitrage betting
   - b. Investment decisions
   - c. Investment strategy
   - d. Inventory investment

5. _____ is the process by which the government, central bank (ii) availability of money, and (iii) cost of money or rate of interest, in order to attain a set of objectives oriented towards the growth and stability of the economy. Monetary theory provides insight into how to craft optimal _____.

   _____ is referred to as either being an expansionary policy where an expansionary policy increases the total supply of money in the economy, and a contractionary policy decreases the total money supply.

   - a. Monetary policy
   - b. 100-year flood
   - c. 1921 recession
   - d. 130-30 fund

Chapter 17. Expectations, Output, and Policy

6. _____ refers to the objective and subjective components of the believability of a source or message.

Traditionally, _____ has two key components: trustworthiness and expertise, which both have objective and subjective components. Trustworthiness is a based more on subjective factors, but can include objective measurements such as established reliability.

a. 100-year flood
b. 130-30 fund
c. 1921 recession
d. Credibility

7. In economics, _____ means that people form their expectations about what will happen in the future based on what has happened in the past. For example, if inflation has been higher than expected in the past, people would revise expectations for the future.

One simple version of _____ is stated in the following equation, where p^e is the next year's rate of inflation that is currently expected; p^e_{-1} is this year's rate of inflation that was expected last year; and p is this year's actual rate of inflation:

$$p^e = p^e_{-1} + \lambda(p_{-1} - p^e_{-1})$$

With λ is between 0 and 1, this says that current expectations of future inflation reflect past expectations and an 'error-adjustment' term, in which current expectations are raised (or lowered) according to the gap between actual inflation and previous expectations.

a. Economic interdependence
b. AD-IA Model
c. Investment-specific technological progress
d. Adaptive expectations

8. _____ is an assumption used in many contemporary macroeconomic models, and also in other areas of contemporary economics and game theory and in other applications of rational choice theory.

Since most macroeconomic models today study decisions over many periods, the expectations of workers, consumers, and firms about future economic conditions are an essential part of the model. How to model these expectations has long been controversial, and it is well known that the macroeconomic predictions of the model may differ depending on the assumptions made about expectations

a. Minimum wage
b. Potential output
c. Balanced-growth equilibrium
d. Rational expectations

9. _____ or government expenditure is classified by economists into three main types. Government purchases of goods and services for current use are classed as government consumption. Government purchases of goods and services intended to create future benefits, such as infrastructure investment or research spending, are classed as government investment.

a. 130-30 fund
b. Government spending
c. 1921 recession
d. 100-year flood

Chapter 18. Openness in Goods and Financial Markets

1. In financial accounting, the _____ is one of the accounts in shareholders' equity. Sole proprietorships have a single _____ in the owner's equity. Partnerships maintain a _____ for each of the partners.
   a. Capital account
   b. Compensation of employees
   c. Net national product
   d. Current account

2. _____ is a type of trade policy that allows traders to act and transact without interference from government. Thus, the policy permits trading partners mutual gains from trade, with goods and services produced according to the theory of comparative advantage.

   Under a _____ policy, prices are a reflection of true supply and demand, and are the sole determinant of resource allocation.

   a. 100-year flood
   b. 130-30 fund
   c. 1921 recession
   d. Free Trade

3. The _____ is a trilateral trade bloc in North America created by the governments of the United States, Canada, and Mexico. The agreement creating the trade bloc came into force on January 1, 1994. It superseded the Canada-United States Free Trade Agreement between the U.S. and Canada.
   a. Case-Shiller Home Price Indices
   b. Demand-side technologies
   c. Federal Reserve Bank Notes
   d. North American Free Trade Agreement

4. A _____ is a duty imposed on goods when they are moved across a political boundary. They are usually associated with protectionism, the economic policy of restraining trade between nations. For political reasons, _____s are usually imposed on imported goods, although they may also be imposed on exported goods.
   a. Tariff
   b. 130-30 fund
   c. 1921 recession
   d. 100-year flood

5. In economics, a _____ is a mechanism that allows people to easily buy and sell (trade) financial securities (such as stocks and bonds), commodities (such as precious metals or agricultural goods), and other fungible items of value at low transaction costs and at prices that reflect the efficient-market hypothesis.

   _____s have evolved significantly over several hundred years and are undergoing constant innovation to improve liquidity.

   Both general markets (where many commodities are traded) and specialized markets (where only one commodity is traded) exist.

   a. Market anomaly
   b. Noise trader
   c. Convertible arbitrage
   d. Financial market

6. A _____ is an object whose consumption increases the utility of the consumer, for which the quantity demanded exceeds the quantity supplied at zero price. _____s are usually modeled as having diminishing marginal utility. The first individual purchase has high utility; the second has less.
   a. Merit good
   b. Pie method
   c. Good
   d. Composite good

Chapter 18. Openness in Goods and Financial Markets

7. In economics, an _____ is any good or commodity, transported from one country to another country in a legitimate fashion, typically for use in trade. _____ goods or services are provided to foreign consumers by domestic producers. _____ is an important part of international trade.
   a. ACEA agreement
   b. ACCRA Cost of Living Index
   c. AD-IA Model
   d. Export

8. In economics, an _____ is any good (e.g. a commodity) or service brought into one country from another country in a legitimate fashion, typically for use in trade. It is a good that is brought in from another country for sale. _____ goods or services are provided to domestic consumers by foreign producers. An _____ in the receiving country is an export to the sending country.
   a. Import
   b. Economic integration
   c. Incoterms
   d. Import quota

9. Economics:

   - _____, the desire to own something and the ability to pay for it
   - _____ curve, a graphic representation of a _____ schedule
   - _____ deposit, the money in checking accounts
   - _____ pull theory, the theory that inflation occurs when _____ for goods and services exceeds existing supplies
   - _____ schedule, a table that lists the quantity of a good a person will buy it each different price
   - _____ side economics, the school of economics at believes government spending and tax cuts open economy by raising _____

   a. Demand
   b. Production
   c. McKesson ' Robbins scandal
   d. Variability

10. The _____ or gross domestic income (GDI), a basic measure of an economy's economic performance, is the market value of all final goods and services produced within the borders of a nation in a year. _____ can be defined in three ways, all of which are conceptually identical. First, it is equal to the total expenditures for all final goods and services produced within the country in a stipulated period of time (usually a 365-day year.)
    a. Monopolistic competition
    b. Market structure
    c. Countercyclical
    d. Gross domestic product

11. In finance, the _____s between two currencies specifies how much one currency is worth in terms of the other. It is the value of a foreign natione;s currency in terms of the home natione;s currency. For example an _____ of 102 Japanese yen to the United States dollar means that JPY 102 is worth the same as USD 1.
    a. Interbank market
    b. Exchange rate
    c. ACEA agreement
    d. ACCRA Cost of Living Index

12. _____ is a term used in accounting relating to the increase in value of an asset. In this sense it is the reverse of depreciation, which measures the fall in value of assets over their normal life-time.

    _____ is a rise of a currency in a floating exchange rate.

a. ACEA agreement
b. Appreciation
c. AD-IA Model
d. ACCRA Cost of Living Index

13. _____ is money accepted for exchange of goods in an economy. The prevalence of one money over another arises, usually, when a government designates through decrees that the government shall accept only particular notes and coins in payment for taxes. Typically, money of _____ consists of stamped coins and minted paper bills.
   a. Totnes pound
   b. Local currency
   c. Security thread
   d. Currency

14. _____ is a term used in accounting, economics and finance to spread the cost of an asset over the span of several years.

In simple words we can say that _____ is the reduction in the value of an asset due to usage, passage of time, wear and tear, technological outdating or obsolescence, depletion, inadequacy, rot, rust, decay or other such factors.

In accounting, _____ is a term used to describe any method of attributing the historical or purchase cost of an asset across its useful life, roughly corresponding to normal wear and tear.

   a. Salvage value
   b. Net income per employee
   c. Depreciation
   d. Historical cost

15. _____ is a reduction in the value of a currency with respect to other monetary units. In common modern usage, it specifically implies an official lowering of the value of a country's currency within a fixed exchange rate system, by which the monetary authority formally sets a new fixed rate with respect to a foreign reference currency. In contrast, (currency) depreciation is used for the unofficial decrease in the exchange rate in a floating exchange rate system.
   a. Texas redbacks
   b. Reserve currency
   c. Petrodollar recycling
   d. Devaluation

16. A _____, sometimes called a pegged exchange rate, is a type of exchange rate regime wherein a currency's value is matched to the value of another single currency or to a basket of other currencies such as gold.

A _____ is usually used to stabilize the value of a currency, vis-a-vis the currency it is pegged to. This facilitates trade and investments between the two countries, and is especially useful for small economies where external trade forms a large part of their GDP.

   a. Law of supply
   b. Monetary economics
   c. Fixed exchange rate
   d. Leading indicators

17. The _____ was a worldwide economic downturn starting in most places in 1929 and ending at different times in the 1930s or early 1940s for different countries. It was the largest and most important economic depression in the 20th century, and is used in the 21st century as an example of how far the world's economy can fall. The _____ originated in the United States; historians most often use as a starting date the stock market crash on October 29, 1929, known as Black Tuesday.

a. Great Depression
b. British Empire Economic Conference
c. Jarrow March
d. Wall Street Crash of 1929

18. _____ means a rise of a price of goods or products. This term is specially used as _____ of a currency, where it means a rise of currency to the relation with a foreign currency in a fixed exchange rate. In floating exchange rate correct term would be appreciation.

a. Deglobalization
b. Legal monopoly
c. Death spiral financing
d. Revaluation

19. _____ is the loss of value of a country's currency with respect to one or more foreign reference currencies, typically in a floating exchange rate system. It is most often used for the unofficial increase of the exchange rate due to market forces, though sometimes it appears interchangeably with devaluation. Its opposite is called appreciation.

a. Fed Shreds
b. Hero Card
c. Quote currency
d. Currency Depreciation

20. In economics, the _____ measures the payments that flow between any individual country and all other countries. It is used to summarize all international economic transactions for that country during a specific time period, usually a year. The _____ is determined by the country's exports and imports of goods, services, and financial capital, as well as financial transfers.

a. Skyscraper Index
b. Gross domestic product per barrel
c. Gross world product
d. Balance of payments

21. A _____ is the transfer of wealth from one party (such as a person or company) to another. A _____ is usually made in exchange for the provision of goods, services or both, or to fulfill a legal obligation.

The simplest and oldest form of _____ is barter, the exchange of one good or service for another.

a. Soft count
b. Going concern
c. Payment
d. Social gravity

22. In economics, the _____ is one of the two primary components of the balance of payments, the other being the capital account. It is the sum of the balance of trade (exports minus imports of goods and services), net factor income (such as interest and dividends) and net transfer payments (such as foreign aid.)

$$\text{Current account} = \text{Balance of trade} \\ + \text{Net factor income from abroad} \\ + \text{Net unilateral transfers from abroad}$$

The _____ balance is one of two major metrics of the nature of a country's foreign trade (the other being the net capital outflow.)

a. Compensation of employees
b. Gross private domestic investment
c. National Income and Product Accounts
d. Current account

Chapter 18. Openness in Goods and Financial Markets

23. _____ is an accounting term which frequently appears as a balance sheet item as a component of shareholders' equity. _____ is used to account for any funds the issuing firm has received over and above the par value of the common stock. It may also be used to account for any gains the firm may derive from selling treasury stock, although this is less commonly seen.

   a. Malinvestment
   b. Direct Registration System
   c. Capital Surplus
   d. National market system plan

24. In business and accounting, _____ are everything of value that is owned by a person or company. It is a claim on the property your income of a borrower. The balance sheet of a firm records the monetary value of the _____ owned by the firm.

   a. Amortization schedule
   b. Assets
   c. ACEA agreement
   d. ACCRA Cost of Living Index

25. A variety of measures of national income and output are used in economics to estimate total economic activity in a country or region, including gross domestic product (GDP), _____ , and net national income (NNI.)

There are three main ways of calculating these numbers; the output approach, the income approach and the expenditure approach. In theory, the three must yield the same, because total expenditures on goods and services must equal the total income paid to the producers (GNI), and that must also equal the total value of the output of goods and services (_____.)

   a. Household final consumption expenditure
   b. Gross national product
   c. Gross world product
   d. Purchasing power parity

26. _____ is a fee paid on borrowed assets. It is the price paid for the use of borrowed money , or, money earned by deposited funds . Assets that are sometimes lent with _____ include money, shares, consumer goods through hire purchase, major assets such as aircraft, and even entire factories in finance lease arrangements.

   a. Internal debt
   b. Asset protection
   c. Insolvency
   d. Interest

27. An _____ is the price a borrower pays for the use of money they do not own, for instance a small company might borrow from a bank to kick start their business, and the return a lender receives for deferring the use of funds, by lending it to the borrower. _____s are normally expressed as a percentage rate over the period of one year.

_____s targets are also a vital tool of monetary policy and are used to control variables like investment, inflation, and unemployment.

   a. Interest rate
   b. Arrow-Debreu model
   c. Enterprise value
   d. ACCRA Cost of Living Index

28. In finance, a _____ is a debt security, in which the authorized issuer owes the holders a debt and, depending on the terms of the _____, is obliged to pay interest (the coupon) and/or to repay the principal at a later date, termed maturity. A _____ is a formal contract to repay borrowed money with interest at fixed intervals.

Thus a _____ is like a loan: the issuer is the borrower (debtor), the holder is the lender (creditor), and the coupon is the interest.

a. Callable
c. Zero-coupon

b. Prize Bond
d. Bond

Chapter 19. The Goods Market in an Open Economy

1. _____ is a common concept in economics, and gives rise to derived concepts such as consumer debt. Generally _____ is defined by opposition to production. But the precise definition can vary because different schools of economists define production quite differently.
   a. Federal Reserve Bank Notes
   b. Cash or share options
   c. Foreclosure data providers
   d. Consumption

2. Economics:

   - _____, the desire to own something and the ability to pay for it
   - _____ curve, a graphic representation of a _____ schedule
   - _____ deposit, the money in checking accounts
   - _____ pull theory, the theory that inflation occurs when _____ for goods and services exceeds existing supplies
   - _____ schedule, a table that lists the quantity of a good a person will buy it each different price
   - _____ side economics, the school of economics at believes government spending and tax cuts open economy by raising _____

   a. McKesson ' Robbins scandal
   b. Demand
   c. Production
   d. Variability

3. A _____ is an object whose consumption increases the utility of the consumer, for which the quantity demanded exceeds the quantity supplied at zero price. _____s are usually modeled as having diminishing marginal utility. The first individual purchase has high utility; the second has less.
   a. Good
   b. Pie method
   c. Merit good
   d. Composite good

4. _____ or government expenditure is classified by economists into three main types. Government purchases of goods and services for current use are classed as government consumption. Government purchases of goods and services intended to create future benefits, such as infrastructure investment or research spending, are classed as government investment.
   a. 100-year flood
   b. Government spending
   c. 1921 recession
   d. 130-30 fund

5. In economics, _____ is the total demand for final goods and services in the economy (Y) at a given time and price level. It is the amount of goods and services in the economy that will be purchased at all possible price levels. This is the demand for the gross domestic product of a country when inventory levels are static.
   a. Aggregation problem
   b. Aggregate supply
   c. Aggregate expenditure
   d. Aggregate demand

6. In algebra, a _____ is a function depending on n that associates a scalar, det(A), to an n×n square matrix A. The fundamental geometric meaning of a _____ is a scale factor for measure when A is regarded as a linear transformation. _____s are important both in calculus, where they enter the substitution rule for several variables, and in multilinear algebra.

   For a fixed nonnegative integer n, there is a unique _____ function for the n×n matrices over any commutative ring R. In particular, this function exists when R is the field of real or complex numbers.

Chapter 19. The Goods Market in an Open Economy

a. 130-30 fund
b. 100-year flood
c. 1921 recession
d. Determinant

7. An _____ is an economy in which people, including businesses, can trade in goods and services with other people and businesses in the international community at large. This contrasts with a closed economy in which international trade cannot take place.

The act of selling goods or services to a foreign country is called exporting.

a. Attention work
b. Open economy
c. Indicative planning
d. Information economy

8. In economics, an _____ is any good or commodity, transported from one country to another country in a legitimate fashion, typically for use in trade. _____ goods or services are provided to foreign consumers by domestic producers. _____ is an important part of international trade.

a. ACCRA Cost of Living Index
b. AD-IA Model
c. ACEA agreement
d. Export

9. In economics, an _____ is any good (e.g. a commodity) or service brought into one country from another country in a legitimate fashion, typically for use in trade.It is a good that is brought in from another country for sale. _____ goods or services are provided to domestic consumers by foreign producers. An _____ in the receiving country is an export to the sending country.

a. Import
b. Incoterms
c. Economic integration
d. Import quota

10. The term _____ refers to government debt, expenditures and revenues, or to finance (particularly financial revenue) in general.

- _____ deficit is the budget deficit of federal or local government
- _____ policy is the discretionary spending of governments. Contrasts with monetary policy.
- _____ year and _____ quarter are reporting periods for firms and other agencies.

a. Drawdown
b. Procter ' Gamble
c. Bucket shop
d. Fiscal

11. In economics, _____ is the use of government spending and revenue collection to influence the economy.

_____ can be contrasted with the other main type of economic policy, monetary policy, which attempts to stabilize the economy by controlling interest rates and the supply of money. The two main instruments of _____ are government spending and taxation.

a. 100-year flood
b. Fiscalism
c. Sustainable investment rule
d. Fiscal policy

Chapter 19. The Goods Market in an Open Economy

12. The balance of trade (or net exports, sometimes symbolized as NX) is the difference between the monetary value of exports and imports in an economy over a certain period of time. It is the relationship between a nation's imports and exports. A favorable balance of trade is known as a trade surplus and consists of exporting more than is imported; an unfavorable balance of trade is known as a _____ or, informally, a trade gap.
    a. Demographics of India
    b. Complementary asset
    c. Trade deficit
    d. Computational economic

13. The _____ is an economic and political union of 27 member states, located primarily in Europe. It was established by the Treaty of Maastricht on 1 November 1993, upon the foundations of the pre-existing European Economic Community. With a population of almost 500 million, the _____ generates an estimated 30% share (US$18.4 trillion in 2008) of the nominal gross world product.
    a. ACEA agreement
    b. ACCRA Cost of Living Index
    c. European Union
    d. European Court of Justice

14. _____ is a branch of applied mathematics that is used in the social sciences (most notably economics), biology, engineering, political science, international relations, computer science, and philosophy. _____ attempts to mathematically capture behavior in strategic situations, in which an individual's success in making choices depends on the choices of others. While initially developed to analyze competitions in which one individual does better at another's expense (zero sum games), it has been expanded to treat a wide class of interactions, which are classified according to several criteria.
    a. Discriminatory price auction
    b. Dollar auction
    c. Proper equilibrium
    d. Game theory

15. _____ is a term used in accounting, economics and finance to spread the cost of an asset over the span of several years.

In simple words we can say that _____ is the reduction in the value of an asset due to usage, passage of time, wear and tear, technological outdating or obsolescence, depletion, inadequacy, rot, rust, decay or other such factors.

In accounting, _____ is a term used to describe any method of attributing the historical or purchase cost of an asset across its useful life, roughly corresponding to normal wear and tear.

    a. Salvage value
    b. Historical cost
    c. Net income per employee
    d. Depreciation

16. In finance, the _____s between two currencies specifies how much one currency is worth in terms of the other. It is the value of a foreign natione;s currency in terms of the home natione;s currency. For example an _____ of 102 Japanese yen to the United States dollar means that JPY 102 is worth the same as USD 1.
    a. ACCRA Cost of Living Index
    b. Interbank market
    c. ACEA agreement
    d. Exchange rate

17. In economics, the _____ is one of the two primary components of the balance of payments, the other being the capital account. It is the sum of the balance of trade (exports minus imports of goods and services), net factor income (such as interest and dividends) and net transfer payments (such as foreign aid.)

$$\text{Current account} = \text{Balance of trade}$$
$$+ \text{ Net factor income from abroad}$$
$$+ \text{ Net unilateral transfers from abroad}$$

The _____ balance is one of two major metrics of the nature of a country's foreign trade (the other being the net capital outflow.)

a. Compensation of employees
b. Gross private domestic investment
c. National Income and Product Accounts
d. Current account

18. The _____ refers to the change in import expenditure that occurs with a change in disposable income (income after taxes and transfers.) For example, if a household earns one extra dollar of disposable income, and the _____ is 0.2, then of that dollar, the household will spend 20 cents of that dollar on imported goods and services.

Mathematically, the _____ (MPI) function is expressed as the derivative of the import (I) function with respect to disposable income (Y.)

a. Hodrick-Prescott filter
b. Complex multiplier
c. Minimum wage
d. Marginal propensity to import

Chapter 20. Output, the Interest Rate, and the Exchange Rate

1. The _____ is an economic model first set forth by Robert Mundell and Marcus Fleming. The model is an extension of the IS-LM model. Whereas IS-LM deals with economy under autarky, the _____ tries to describe a small open economy.
    a. Harrod-Domar model
    b. Mundell-Fleming model
    c. Rostovian take-off model
    d. Representative agent

2. A _____ is an object whose consumption increases the utility of the consumer, for which the quantity demanded exceeds the quantity supplied at zero price. _____s are usually modeled as having diminishing marginal utility. The first individual purchase has high utility; the second has less.
    a. Composite good
    b. Good
    c. Merit good
    d. Pie method

3. In economics, economic equilibrium is simply a state of the world where economic forces are balanced and in the absence of external influences the (equilibrium) values of economic variables will not change. It is the point at which quantity demanded and quantity supplied are equal. _____, for example, refers to a condition where a market price is established through competition such that the amount of goods or services sought by buyers is equal to the amount of goods or services produced by sellers.
    a. Regulated market
    b. Product-Market Growth Matrix
    c. Marketization
    d. Market Equilibrium

4. In finance, a _____ is a debt security, in which the authorized issuer owes the holders a debt and, depending on the terms of the _____, is obliged to pay interest (the coupon) and/or to repay the principal at a later date, termed maturity. A _____ is a formal contract to repay borrowed money with interest at fixed intervals.

    Thus a _____ is like a loan: the issuer is the borrower (debtor), the holder is the lender (creditor), and the coupon is the interest.

    a. Bond
    b. Prize Bond
    c. Zero-coupon
    d. Callable

5. A _____, reserve bank, or monetary authority is the entity responsible for the monetary policy of a country or of a group of member states. It is a bank that can lend money to other banks in times of need. Its primary responsibility is to maintain the stability of the national currency and money supply, but more active duties include controlling subsidized-loan interest rates, and acting as a lender of last resort to the banking sector during times of financial crisis (private banks often being integral to the national financial system.)
    a. 100-year flood
    b. 1921 recession
    c. 130-30 fund
    d. Central bank

6. In economics, a _____ is a mechanism that allows people to easily buy and sell (trade) financial securities (such as stocks and bonds), commodities (such as precious metals or agricultural goods), and other fungible items of value at low transaction costs and at prices that reflect the efficient-market hypothesis.

    _____s have evolved significantly over several hundred years and are undergoing constant innovation to improve liquidity.

    Both general markets (where many commodities are traded) and specialized markets (where only one commodity is traded) exist.

a. Noise trader
b. Market anomaly
c. Convertible arbitrage
d. Financial market

7. In economics, the _____ measures the payments that flow between any individual country and all other countries. It is used to summarize all international economic transactions for that country during a specific time period, usually a year. The _____ is determined by the country's exports and imports of goods, services, and financial capital, as well as financial transfers.

   a. Gross world product
   b. Gross domestic product per barrel
   c. Balance of payments
   d. Skyscraper Index

8. A _____ is the transfer of wealth from one party (such as a person or company) to another. A _____ is usually made in exchange for the provision of goods, services or both, or to fulfill a legal obligation.

   The simplest and oldest form of _____ is barter, the exchange of one good or service for another.

   a. Soft count
   b. Going concern
   c. Payment
   d. Social gravity

9. _____ is a fee paid on borrowed assets. It is the price paid for the use of borrowed money, or, money earned by deposited funds. Assets that are sometimes lent with _____ include money, shares, consumer goods through hire purchase, major assets such as aircraft, and even entire factories in finance lease arrangements.

   a. Internal debt
   b. Insolvency
   c. Asset protection
   d. Interest

10. The term _____ refers to government debt, expenditures and revenues, or to finance (particularly financial revenue) in general.

    - _____ deficit is the budget deficit of federal or local government
    - _____ policy is the discretionary spending of governments. Contrasts with monetary policy.
    - _____ year and _____ quarter are reporting periods for firms and other agencies.

    a. Fiscal
    b. Drawdown
    c. Procter ' Gamble
    d. Bucket shop

11. In economics, _____ is the use of government spending and revenue collection to influence the economy.

    _____ can be contrasted with the other main type of economic policy, monetary policy, which attempts to stabilize the economy by controlling interest rates and the supply of money. The two main instruments of _____ are government spending and taxation.

    a. Fiscalism
    b. 100-year flood
    c. Sustainable investment rule
    d. Fiscal policy

Chapter 20. Output, the Interest Rate, and the Exchange Rate

12. An _____ is an economy in which people, including businesses, can trade in goods and services with other people and businesses in the international community at large. This contrasts with a closed economy in which international trade cannot take place.

The act of selling goods or services to a foreign country is called exporting.

 a. Information economy
 b. Indicative planning
 c. Open economy
 d. Attention work

13. A _____, sometimes called a pegged exchange rate, is a type of exchange rate regime wherein a currency's value is matched to the value of another single currency or to a basket of other currencies such as gold.

A _____ is usually used to stabilize the value of a currency, vis-a-vis the currency it is pegged to. This facilitates trade and investments between the two countries, and is especially useful for small economies where external trade forms a large part of their GDP.

 a. Leading indicators
 b. Law of supply
 c. Monetary economics
 d. Fixed exchange rate

14. _____ is the process by which the government, central bank (ii) availability of money, and (iii) cost of money or rate of interest, in order to attain a set of objectives oriented towards the growth and stability of the economy. Monetary theory provides insight into how to craft optimal _____.

_____ is referred to as either being an expansionary policy where an expansionary policy increases the total supply of money in the economy, and a contractionary policy decreases the total money supply.

 a. 1921 recession
 b. Monetary policy
 c. 100-year flood
 d. 130-30 fund

15. _____ refers to the objective and subjective components of the believability of a source or message.

Traditionally, _____ has two key components: trustworthiness and expertise, which both have objective and subjective components. Trustworthiness is a based more on subjective factors, but can include objective measurements such as established reliability.

 a. 130-30 fund
 b. 1921 recession
 c. 100-year flood
 d. Credibility

16. In finance, the _____s between two currencies specifies how much one currency is worth in terms of the other. It is the value of a foreign natione;s currency in terms of the home natione;s currency. For example an _____ of 102 Japanese yen to the United States dollar means that JPY 102 is worth the same as USD 1.

 a. ACEA agreement
 b. ACCRA Cost of Living Index
 c. Interbank market
 d. Exchange rate

17. _____ is money accepted for exchange of goods in an economy. The prevalence of one money over another arises, usually, when a government designates through decrees that the government shall accept only particular notes and coins in payment for taxes. Typically, money of _____ consists of stamped coins and minted paper bills.
   a. Local currency
   b. Totnes pound
   c. Security thread
   d. Currency

18. The _____ was a worldwide economic downturn starting in most places in 1929 and ending at different times in the 1930s or early 1940s for different countries. It was the largest and most important economic depression in the 20th century, and is used in the 21st century as an example of how far the world's economy can fall. The _____ originated in the United States; historians most often use as a starting date the stock market crash on October 29, 1929, known as Black Tuesday.
   a. British Empire Economic Conference
   b. Wall Street Crash of 1929
   c. Jarrow March
   d. Great Depression

19. A _____ occurs when an entity spends more money than it takes in. The opposite of a _____ is a budget surplus. Debt is essentially an accumulated flow of deficits.
   a. Funding body
   b. Lump-sum tax
   c. Public Financial Management
   d. Budget deficit

20. A consumer price index (_____) is a measure of the average price of consumer goods and services purchased by households. A consumer price index measures a price change for a constant market basket of goods and services from one period to the next within the same area (city, region, or nation.) It is a price index determined by measuring the price of a standard group of goods meant to represent the typical market basket of a typical urban consumer.
   a. CPI
   b. Lipstick index
   c. Hedonic price index
   d. Cost-of-living index

21. _____ is a reduction in the value of a currency with respect to other monetary units. In common modern usage, it specifically implies an official lowering of the value of a country's currency within a fixed exchange rate system, by which the monetary authority formally sets a new fixed rate with respect to a foreign reference currency. In contrast, (currency) depreciation is used for the unofficial decrease in the exchange rate in a floating exchange rate system.
   a. Texas redbacks
   b. Petrodollar recycling
   c. Reserve currency
   d. Devaluation

22. _____ means a rise of a price of goods or products. This term is specially used as _____ of a currency, where it means a rise of currency to the relation with a foreign currency in a fixed exchange rate. In floating exchange rate correct term would be appreciation.
   a. Legal monopoly
   b. Revaluation
   c. Deglobalization
   d. Death spiral financing

23. The balance of trade (or net exports, sometimes symbolized as NX) is the difference between the monetary value of exports and imports in an economy over a certain period of time. It is the relationship between a nation's imports and exports. A favorable balance of trade is known as a trade surplus and consists of exporting more than is imported; an unfavorable balance of trade is known as a _____ or, informally, a trade gap.
   a. Computational economic
   b. Complementary asset
   c. Demographics of India
   d. Trade deficit

Chapter 20. Output, the Interest Rate, and the Exchange Rate

24. The _____ hypothesis is a concept from macroeconomics that contends that there is a strong link between a national economy's current account balance and its government budget balance. As an example, it is hypothesized that a large budget deficit leads to a large current account deficit. The theory goes as follows:

Y = C + I + G + NX

where Y represents National Income or GDP, C is consumption, I is investment, G is government spending and NX stands for net exports.

a. 100-year flood
b. Power of the purse
c. Public-private partnership
d. Twin deficits

25. The _____ is the official currency of 16 of the 27 member states of the European Union (EU.) The states, known collectively as the Eurozone, are Austria, Belgium, Cyprus, Finland, France, Germany, Greece, Ireland, Italy, Luxembourg, Malta, the Netherlands, Portugal, Slovakia, Slovenia, and Spain. The currency is also used in a further five European countries, with and without formal agreements and is consequently used daily by some 327 million Europeans.

a. Import and Export Price Indices
b. IRS Code 3401
c. Equity capital market
d. Euro

26. _____ was an arrangement established in 1979 under the Jenkins European Commission where most nations of the European Economic Community (EEC) linked their currencies to prevent large fluctuations relative to one another.

After the collapse of the Bretton Woods system in 1971, most of the EEC countries agreed in 1972 to maintain stable exchange rates by preventing exchange fluctuations of more than 2.25% (the European 'currency snake'.) In March 1979, this system was replaced by the _____, and the European Currency Unit (ECU) was defined.

a. European Monetary Union
b. European Monetary System
c. Euro Interbank Offered Rate
d. Exchange rate mechanism

27. A _____ secures the proper functioning of money by regulating economic agents, transaction types, and money supply.

_____s are traditionally formed by the policy decisions of individual governments and administrated as a domestic economic issue.

The current trend, however, is to use international trade and investment to alter the policy and legislation of individual governments.

a. Consumer basket
b. Monetary System
c. Financial rand
d. Netting

28. In financial accounting, the _____ is one of the accounts in shareholders' equity. Sole proprietorships have a single _____ in the owner's equity. Partnerships maintain a _____ for each of the partners.

a. Compensation of employees
b. Capital account
c. Net national product
d. Current account

Chapter 21. Exchange Rate Regimes

1. In economics, _____ is the total demand for final goods and services in the economy (Y) at a given time and price level. It is the amount of goods and services in the economy that will be purchased at all possible price levels. This is the demand for the gross domestic product of a country when inventory levels are static.
   a. Aggregate expenditure
   b. Aggregation problem
   c. Aggregate supply
   d. Aggregate demand

2. Economics:

   - _____, the desire to own something and the ability to pay for it
   - _____ curve, a graphic representation of a _____ schedule
   - _____ deposit, the money in checking accounts
   - _____ pull theory, the theory that inflation occurs when _____ for goods and services exceeds existing supplies
   - _____ schedule, a table that lists the quantity of a good a person will buy it each different price
   - _____ side economics, the school of economics at believes government spending and tax cuts open economy by raising _____

   a. Variability
   b. Demand
   c. Production
   d. McKesson ' Robbins scandal

3. In finance, the _____s between two currencies specifies how much one currency is worth in terms of the other. It is the value of a foreign natione;s currency in terms of the home natione;s currency. For example an _____ of 102 Japanese yen to the United States dollar means that JPY 102 is worth the same as USD 1.
   a. Exchange rate
   b. Interbank market
   c. ACCRA Cost of Living Index
   d. ACEA agreement

4. In economics, a _____ is a mechanism that allows people to easily buy and sell (trade) financial securities (such as stocks and bonds), commodities (such as precious metals or agricultural goods), and other fungible items of value at low transaction costs and at prices that reflect the efficient-market hypothesis.

   _____s have evolved significantly over several hundred years and are undergoing constant innovation to improve liquidity.

   Both general markets (where many commodities are traded) and specialized markets (where only one commodity is traded) exist.

   a. Noise trader
   b. Market anomaly
   c. Convertible arbitrage
   d. Financial market

5. A _____, sometimes called a pegged exchange rate, is a type of exchange rate regime wherein a currency's value is matched to the value of another single currency or to a basket of other currencies such as gold.

   A _____ is usually used to stabilize the value of a currency, vis-a-vis the currency it is pegged to. This facilitates trade and investments between the two countries, and is especially useful for small economies where external trade forms a large part of their GDP.

a. Law of supply
b. Monetary economics
c. Leading indicators
d. Fixed exchange rate

6. _____ is a reduction in the value of a currency with respect to other monetary units. In common modern usage, it specifically implies an official lowering of the value of a country's currency within a fixed exchange rate system, by which the monetary authority formally sets a new fixed rate with respect to a foreign reference currency. In contrast, (currency) depreciation is used for the unofficial decrease in the exchange rate in a floating exchange rate system.

a. Petrodollar recycling
b. Devaluation
c. Reserve currency
d. Texas redbacks

7. The _____ was a worldwide economic downturn starting in most places in 1929 and ending at different times in the 1930s or early 1940s for different countries. It was the largest and most important economic depression in the 20th century, and is used in the 21st century as an example of how far the world's economy can fall. The _____ originated in the United States; historians most often use as a starting date the stock market crash on October 29, 1929, known as Black Tuesday.

a. Great Depression
b. British Empire Economic Conference
c. Wall Street Crash of 1929
d. Jarrow March

8. _____, 1st Baron Keynes was a renowned economist from Britain whose many ideas on economic and political theories as well as on many governments' monetary policies influenced America. He advocated a government that played an active role in the lives of people regarding business, economy, etc. In this role, the government would use fiscal measures to reduce the consequences of recessions, economic depressions and booms.

a. Adolph Fischer
b. Adolf Hitler
c. Adam Smith
d. John Maynard Keynes

9. The _____ is a monetary system in which a region's common medium of exchange are paper notes that are normally freely convertible into pre-set, fixed quantities of gold. The _____ is not currently used by any government, having been replaced completely by fiat currency. Gold certificates were used as paper currency in the United States from 1882 to 1933, these certificates were freely convertable into gold coins.

In the 1790s Britain suffered a massive shortage of silver coinage and ceased to mint larger silver coins.

a. 100-year flood
b. Gold standard
c. 130-30 fund
d. 1921 recession

10. _____ was an arrangement established in 1979 under the Jenkins European Commission where most nations of the European Economic Community (EEC) linked their currencies to prevent large fluctuations relative to one another.

After the collapse of the Bretton Woods system in 1971, most of the EEC countries agreed in 1972 to maintain stable exchange rates by preventing exchange fluctuations of more than 2.25% (the European 'currency snake'.) In March 1979, this system was replaced by the _____, and the European Currency Unit (ECU) was defined.

a. European Monetary Union
b. Exchange rate mechanism
c. Euro Interbank Offered Rate
d. European Monetary System

Chapter 21. Exchange Rate Regimes

11. A _____ secures the proper functioning of money by regulating economic agents, transaction types, and money supply.

_____s are traditionally formed by the policy decisions of individual governments and administrated as a domestic economic issue.

The current trend, however, is to use international trade and investment to alter the policy and legislation of individual governments.

a. Netting
c. Consumer basket
b. Financial rand
d. Monetary System

12. In economics, the _____ is one of the two primary components of the balance of payments, the other being the capital account. It is the sum of the balance of trade (exports minus imports of goods and services), net factor income (such as interest and dividends) and net transfer payments (such as foreign aid.)

$$\text{Current account} = \text{Balance of trade} \\ + \text{Net factor income from abroad} \\ + \text{Net unilateral transfers from abroad}$$

The _____ balance is one of two major metrics of the nature of a country's foreign trade (the other being the net capital outflow.)

a. National Income and Product Accounts
c. Compensation of employees
b. Current account
d. Gross private domestic investment

13. _____ is a fee paid on borrowed assets. It is the price paid for the use of borrowed money, or, money earned by deposited funds. Assets that are sometimes lent with _____ include money, shares, consumer goods through hire purchase, major assets such as aircraft, and even entire factories in finance lease arrangements.

a. Insolvency
c. Internal debt
b. Interest
d. Asset protection

14. An _____ is the price a borrower pays for the use of money they do not own, for instance a small company might borrow from a bank to kick start their business, and the return a lender receives for deferring the use of funds, by lending it to the borrower. _____s are normally expressed as a percentage rate over the period of one year.

_____s targets are also a vital tool of monetary policy and are used to control variables like investment, inflation, and unemployment.

a. Arrow-Debreu model
c. Enterprise value
b. ACCRA Cost of Living Index
d. Interest rate

15. _____ is money accepted for exchange of goods in an economy. The prevalence of one money over another arises, usually, when a government designates through decrees that the government shall accept only particular notes and coins in payment for taxes. Typically, money of _____ consists of stamped coins and minted paper bills.

a. Totnes pound
c. Security thread
b. Local currency
d. Currency

16. The _____ is the official currency of 16 of the 27 member states of the European Union (EU.) The states, known collectively as the Eurozone, are Austria, Belgium, Cyprus, Finland, France, Germany, Greece, Ireland, Italy, Luxembourg, Malta, the Netherlands, Portugal, Slovakia, Slovenia, and Spain. The currency is also used in a further five European countries, with and without formal agreements and is consequently used daily by some 327 million Europeans.

a. IRS Code 3401
c. Equity capital market
b. Import and Export Price Indices
d. Euro

17. _____ is the value on a given date of a future payment or series of future payments, discounted to reflect the time value of money and other factors such as investment risk. _____ calculations are widely used in business and economics to provide a means to compare cash flows at different times on a meaningful 'like to like' basis.

Money value fluctuates over time: $100 today are not worth $100 in five years.

a. Tax shield
c. Present value of costs
b. Future value
d. Present value

18. _____ is the a method of technical and economic research of the systems for purpose to optimize a parity between system's consumer functions or properties and expenses to achieve those functions or properties.

This methodology for continuous perfection of production, industrial technologies, organizational structures was developed by Juryj Sobolev in 1948 at the 'Perm telephone factory'

- 1948 Juryj Sobolev - the first success in application of a method analysis at the 'Perm telephone factory' .
- 1949 - the first application for the invention as result of use of the new method.

Today in economically developed countries practically each enterprise or the company use methodology of the kind of functional-cost analysis as a practice of the quality management, most full satisfying to principles of standards of series ISO 9000.

- Interest of consumer not in products itself, but the advantage which it will receive from its usage.
- The consumer aspires to reduce his expenses
- Functions needed by consumer can be executed in the various ways, and, hence, with various efficiency and expenses. Among possible alternatives of realization of functions exist such in which the parity of quality and the price is the optimal for the consumer.

The goal of _____ is achievement of the highest consumer satisfaction of production at simultaneous decrease in all kinds of industrial expenses Classical _____ has three English synonyms - Value Engineering, Value Management, Value Analysis.

a. Staple financing
c. Function cost analysis
b. Monopoly wage
d. Willingness to pay

Chapter 21. Exchange Rate Regimes

19. A _____, reserve bank, or monetary authority is the entity responsible for the monetary policy of a country or of a group of member states. It is a bank that can lend money to other banks in times of need. Its primary responsibility is to maintain the stability of the national currency and money supply, but more active duties include controlling subsidized-loan interest rates, and acting as a lender of last resort to the banking sector during times of financial crisis (private banks often being integral to the national financial system.)
   a. Central Bank
   b. 130-30 fund
   c. 1921 recession
   d. 100-year flood

20. The _____ is one of the world's most important central banks, responsible for monetary policy covering the 16 member States of the Eurozone. It was established by the European Union (EU) in 1998 with its headquarters in Frankfurt, Germany.

The predecessor to the _____ was the European Monetary Institute .

   a. ACCRA Cost of Living Index
   b. ACEA agreement
   c. European Central Bank
   d. AD-IA Model

21. _____ is sometimes referred to as _____, actually it means Economic Monetary Union.

First ideas of an economic and monetary union in Europe were raised well before establishing the European Communities. For example, already in the League of Nations, Gustav Stresemann asked in 1929 for a European currency (Link) against the background of an increased economic division due to a number of new nation states in Europe after WWI.

   a. European Monetary System
   b. Exchange rate mechanism
   c. Euro Interbank Offered Rate
   d. European Monetary Union

22. The _____ was signed on 7 February 1992 in Maastricht, the Netherlands after final negotiations on 9 December 1991 between the members of the European Community and entered into force on 1 November 1993 during the Delors Commission. It created the European Union and led to the creation of the euro. The _____ has been amended to a degree by later treaties.
   a. Treaties of Rome
   b. Treaty of Amsterdam
   c. Maastricht Treaty
   d. 100-year flood

23. An economic and _____ is a single market with a common currency. It is to be distinguished from a mere currency union , which does not involve a single market. This is the fifth stage of economic integration.
   a. Free trade zone
   b. Customs union
   c. Monetary Union
   d. Commercial invoice

24. A _____ is a monetary authority which is required to maintain a fixed exchange rate with a foreign currency. This policy objective requires the conventional objectives of a central bank to be subordinated to the exchange rate target.

Chapter 21. Exchange Rate Regimes

The main qualities of an orthodox _____ are:

- A _____'s foreign currency reserves must be sufficient to ensure that all holders of its notes and coins (and all banks creditor of a Reserve Account at the _____) can convert them into the reserve currency (usually 110-115% of the monetary base M0.)
- A _____ maintains absolute, unlimited convertibility between its notes and coins and the currency against which they are pegged (the anchor currency), at a fixed rate of exchange, with no restrictions on current-account or capital-account transactions.
- A _____ only earns profit from interests on foreign reserves (less the expense of note-issuing), and does not engage in forward-exchange transactions. These foreign reserves exist (1) because local notes have been issued in exchange, or (2) because commercial banks must by regulation deposit a minimum reserve at the _____. (1) generates a seignorage revenue. (2) is the revenue on minimum reserves (revenue of investment activities less cost of minimum reserves remuneration)
- A _____ has no discretionary powers to effect monetary policy and does not lend to the government. Governments cannot print money, and can only tax or borrow to meet their spending commitments.
- A _____ does not act as a lender of last resort to commercial banks, and does not regulate reserve requirements.
- A _____ does not attempt to manipulate interest rates by establishing a discount rate like a central bank. The peg with the foreign currency tends to keep interest rates and inflation very closely aligned to those in the country against whose currency the peg is fixed.

The _____ in question will no longer issue fiat money but instead will only issue one unit of local currency for each unit (or decided amount) of foreign currency it has in its vault (often a hard currency such as the U.S. dollar or the euro.) The surplus on the balance of payments of that country is reflected by higher deposits local banks hold at the central bank as well as (initially) higher deposits of the (net) exporting firms at their local banks.

a. Petrodollar
c. Reserve currency

b. Currency board
d. Currency competition

25. _____ occurs when the inhabitants of a country use foreign currency in parallel to or instead of the domestic currency.

_____ can occur

- unofficially, when private agents prefer the foreign currency over the domestic currency. They hold for example deposits in the foreign currency because of a bad track record of the local currency.

- semiofficially (or officially bimonetary systems), where foreign currency is legal tender, but plays a secondary role to domestic currency
- officially, when a country ceases to issue the domestic currency and uses only foreign currency. It adopts the foreign currency as legal tender.

The term _____ is not only applied to usage of the United States dollar, but also generally to the use of any foreign currency as the national currency.

a. Dollarization
b. Commodity money
c. World currency
d. Currency board

26. The '_____' is approximately the nominal interest rate minus the inflation rate Since the inflation rate over the course of a loan is not known initially, volatility in inflation represents a risk to both the lender and the borrower.

In economics and finance, an individual who lends money for repayment at a later point in time expects to be compensated for the time value of money, or not having the use of that money while it is lent.

a. Real interest rate
b. Core inflation
c. Cost-push inflation
d. Reflation

Chapter 22. Depressions and Slumps

1. In economics, _____ is a sustained decrease in the general price level of goods and services. _____ occurs when the annual inflation rate falls below zero percent, resulting in an increase in the real value of money -- a negative inflation rate. This should not be confused with disinflation, a slow-down in the inflation rate (i.e. when the inflation decreases, but still remains positive.)
   a. Deflation
   b. Tobit model
   c. Price revolution
   d. Literacy rate

2. _____ is a decrease in the rate of inflation. This phase of the business cycle, in which retailers can no longer pass on higher prices to their customers, often occurs during a recession. In contrast, deflation occurs when prices are actually dropping.
   a. Stealth inflation
   b. Mundell-Tobin effect
   c. Reflation
   d. Disinflation

3. Market _____ is a business, economics or investment term that refers to an asset's ability to be easily converted through an act of buying or selling without causing a significant movement in the price and with minimum loss of value. Money, or cash on hand, is the most liquid asset. An act of exchange of a less liquid asset with a more liquid asset is called liquidation.
   a. 100-year flood
   b. 1921 recession
   c. 130-30 fund
   d. Liquidity

4. The term _____ is used in macroeconomics to refer to a situation where a country's nominal interest rate has been lowered nearly to or equal to zero to avoid a recession, but the liquidity in the market created by these low interest rates does not stimulate the economy to full employment. In this situation, any further increase in the money supply will not stimulate the economy any further. This is because any further injection of liquidity will no longer lower the nominal interest rate, as the nominal interest rate cannot drop below zero.
   a. Liquidity trap
   b. Macroeconomic models
   c. Minimum wage
   d. Robertson lag

5. In economics, _____ is inflation that is very high or 'out of control', a condition in which prices increase rapidly as a currency loses its value. Definitions used by the media vary from a cumulative inflation rate over three years approaching 100% to 'inflation exceeding 50% a month.' In informal usage the term is often applied to much lower rates. As a rule of thumb, normal inflation is reported per year, but _____ is often reported for much shorter intervals, often per month.
   a. 130-30 fund
   b. 1921 recession
   c. 100-year flood
   d. Hyperinflation

6. The _____ was a worldwide economic downturn starting in most places in 1929 and ending at different times in the 1930s or early 1940s for different countries. It was the largest and most important economic depression in the 20th century, and is used in the 21st century as an example of how far the world's economy can fall. The _____ originated in the United States; historians most often use as a starting date the stock market crash on October 29, 1929, known as Black Tuesday.
   a. Wall Street Crash of 1929
   b. Jarrow March
   c. British Empire Economic Conference
   d. Great Depression

7. _____, 1st Baron Keynes was a renowned economist from Britain whose many ideas on economic and political theories as well as on many governments' monetary policies influenced America. He advocated a government that played an active role in the lives of people regarding business, economy, etc. In this role, the government would use fiscal measures to reduce the consequences of recessions, economic depressions and booms.

Chapter 22. Depressions and Slumps

a. Adolph Fischer
c. Adolf Hitler
b. Adam Smith
d. John Maynard Keynes

8. Unemployment occurs when a person is available to work and seeking work but currently without work. The prevalence of unemployment is usually measured using the _____, which is defined as the percentage of those in the labor force who are unemployed. The _____ is also used in economic studies and economic indexes such as the United States' Conference Board's Index of Leading Indicators as a measure of the state of the macroeconomics.
   a. ACEA agreement
   c. Unemployment rate
   b. ACCRA Cost of Living Index
   d. AD-IA Model

9. _____ is a common concept in economics, and gives rise to derived concepts such as consumer debt. Generally _____ is defined by opposition to production. But the precise definition can vary because different schools of economists define production quite differently.
   a. Consumption
   c. Foreclosure data providers
   b. Federal Reserve Bank Notes
   d. Cash or share options

10. A _____, reserve bank, or monetary authority is the entity responsible for the monetary policy of a country or of a group of member states. It is a bank that can lend money to other banks in times of need. Its primary responsibility is to maintain the stability of the national currency and money supply, but more active duties include controlling subsidized-loan interest rates, and acting as a lender of last resort to the banking sector during times of financial crisis (private banks often being integral to the national financial system.)
   a. 130-30 fund
   c. 100-year flood
   b. 1921 recession
   d. Central bank

11. _____ was an American economist, statistician and public intellectual, and a recipient of the Nobel Memorial Prize in Economic Sciences. He is best known among scholars for his theoretical and empirical research, especially consumption analysis, monetary history and theory, and for his demonstration of the complexity of stabilization policy. A global public followed his restatement of a political philosophy that insisted on minimizing the role of government in favor of the private sector.
   a. Adam Smith
   c. Adolph Fischer
   b. Milton Friedman
   d. Adolf Hitler

12. In finance, a _____ is a debt security, in which the authorized issuer owes the holders a debt and, depending on the terms of the _____, is obliged to pay interest (the coupon) and/or to repay the principal at a later date, termed maturity. A _____ is a formal contract to repay borrowed money with interest at fixed intervals.

Thus a _____ is like a loan: the issuer is the borrower (debtor), the holder is the lender (creditor), and the coupon is the interest.

   a. Zero-coupon
   c. Callable
   b. Prize Bond
   d. Bond

13. _____, in economics, is the quantity of money measured in a particular currency and is directly proportional to the price level.

This means, among other things, that if the price level rises by 10%, 10% more money than before is necessary in order to maintain stability. For example, if it costs $20 to buy an item, and the price level increases by 10%, the dollar amount necessary to buy the item increases by 10% (in this case by $2), which brings the total cost of the item to $22.

    a. Nominal money
    c. Limping bimetallism
    b. Silver Thursday
    d. Money of account

14. The _____ consists of a number of economic theories which describe the nature of the firm, company including its existence, its behaviour, and its relationship with the market.

In simplified terms, the _____ aims to answer these questions:

1. Existence - why do firms emerge, why are not all transactions in the economy mediated over the market?
2. Boundaries - why the boundary between firms and the market is located exactly there? Which transactions are performed internally and which are negotiated on the market?
3. Organization - why are firms structured in such specific way? What is the interplay of formal and informal relationships?

Despite looking simple, these questions are not answered by the established economic theory, which usually views firms as given, and treats them as black boxes without any internal structure.

The First World War period saw a change of emphasis in economic theory away from industry-level analysis which mainly included analysing markets to analysis at the level of the firm, as it became increasingly clear that perfect competition was no longer an adequate model of how firms behaved. Economic theory till then had focussed on trying to understand markets alone and there had been little study on understanding why firms or organisations exist.

    a. Policy Ineffectiveness Proposition
    c. Technology gap
    b. Theory of the firm
    d. Khazzoom-Brookes postulate

15. The _____ is a United States government corporation created by the Glass-Steagall Act of 1933. It provides deposit insurance, which guarantees the safety of deposits in member banks, currently up to $250,000 per depositor per bank. Funds in non-interest bearing transaction accounts are fully insured, with no limit, under the temporary Transaction Account Guarantee Program.

    a. Federal Deposit Insurance Corporation
    c. Luxembourg Income Study
    b. Great Leap Forward
    d. Foreign direct investment

16. _____, in law and economics, is a form of risk management primarily used to hedge against the risk of a contingent loss. _____ is defined as the equitable transfer of the risk of a loss, from one entity to another, in exchange for a premium, and can be thought of as a guaranteed small loss to prevent a large, possibly devastating loss. An insurer is a company selling the _____; an insured or policyholder is the person or entity buying the _____.

Chapter 22. Depressions and Slumps

a. AD-IA Model
b. Insurance
c. ACCRA Cost of Living Index
d. ACEA agreement

17. In mathematics, a _____ is a constant multiplicative factor of a certain object. For example, in the expression $9x^2$, the _____ of x^2 is 9.

The object can be such things as a variable, a vector, a function, etc.

a. 1921 recession
b. 100-year flood
c. 130-30 fund
d. Coefficient

18. The term _____ refers to government debt, expenditures and revenues, or to finance (particularly financial revenue) in general.

- _____ deficit is the budget deficit of federal or local government
- _____ policy is the discretionary spending of governments. Contrasts with monetary policy.
- _____ year and _____ quarter are reporting periods for firms and other agencies.

a. Procter ' Gamble
b. Drawdown
c. Bucket shop
d. Fiscal

19. In economics, _____ is the use of government spending and revenue collection to influence the economy.

_____ can be contrasted with the other main type of economic policy, monetary policy, which attempts to stabilize the economy by controlling interest rates and the supply of money. The two main instruments of _____ are government spending and taxation.

a. Fiscal policy
b. 100-year flood
c. Sustainable investment rule
d. Fiscalism

20. _____ is the process by which the government, central bank (ii) availability of money, and (iii) cost of money or rate of interest, in order to attain a set of objectives oriented towards the growth and stability of the economy. Monetary theory provides insight into how to craft optimal _____.

_____ is referred to as either being an expansionary policy where an expansionary policy increases the total supply of money in the economy, and a contractionary policy decreases the total money supply.

a. 130-30 fund
b. 100-year flood
c. 1921 recession
d. Monetary policy

21. _____ refers to the objective and subjective components of the believability of a source or message.

Traditionally, _____ has two key components: trustworthiness and expertise, which both have objective and subjective components. Trustworthiness is a based more on subjective factors, but can include objective measurements such as established reliability.

a. 1921 recession
c. 100-year flood
b. Credibility
d. 130-30 fund

Chapter 23. High Inflation

1. _____s is the social science that studies the production, distribution, and consumption of goods and services. The term _____s comes from the Ancient Greek oá¼°κονομῖα from oá¼¶κος (oikos, 'house') + vÏŒμος (nomos, 'custom' or 'law'), hence 'rules of the house(hold)'. Current _____ models developed out of the broader field of political economy in the late 19th century, owing to a desire to use an empirical approach more akin to the physical sciences.
   a. Opportunity cost
   b. Energy economics
   c. Inflation
   d. Economic

2. In economics, _____ is inflation that is very high or 'out of control', a condition in which prices increase rapidly as a currency loses its value. Definitions used by the media vary from a cumulative inflation rate over three years approaching 100% to 'inflation exceeding 50% a month.' In informal usage the term is often applied to much lower rates. As a rule of thumb, normal inflation is reported per year, but _____ is often reported for much shorter intervals, often per month.
   a. 1921 recession
   b. Hyperinflation
   c. 100-year flood
   d. 130-30 fund

3. A _____ occurs when an entity spends more money than it takes in. The opposite of a _____ is a budget surplus. Debt is essentially an accumulated flow of deficits.
   a. Funding body
   b. Budget deficit
   c. Public Financial Management
   d. Lump-sum tax

4. A _____, reserve bank, or monetary authority is the entity responsible for the monetary policy of a country or of a group of member states. It is a bank that can lend money to other banks in times of need. Its primary responsibility is to maintain the stability of the national currency and money supply, but more active duties include controlling subsidized-loan interest rates, and acting as a lender of last resort to the banking sector during times of financial crisis (private banks often being integral to the national financial system.)
   a. 130-30 fund
   b. Central bank
   c. 1921 recession
   d. 100-year flood

5. In finance, a _____ is a debt security, in which the authorized issuer owes the holders a debt and, depending on the terms of the _____, is obliged to pay interest (the coupon) and/or to repay the principal at a later date, termed maturity. A _____ is a formal contract to repay borrowed money with interest at fixed intervals.

   Thus a _____ is like a loan: the issuer is the borrower (debtor), the holder is the lender (creditor), and the coupon is the interest.

   a. Bond
   b. Prize Bond
   c. Zero-coupon
   d. Callable

6. _____ is the process by which money is produced or issued. There are three different ways to create money:

   - manufacturing a new monetary unit, such as paper currency or metal coins (_____)
   - loaning out a physical monetary unit multiple times through fractional-reserve lending (credit creation)
   - buying of government securities or other financial instruments by central bank through Open market operations (electronic creation)

   Coins are produced by manufacturing metal in a factory called a mint.

   Banknotes and bank account balances are financial securities issued by a bank.

Similarly, money destruction, i.e., the reverse of _____, can occur in two different ways, depending on how the money was created.

a. Monetary policy of Sweden
b. Second-round effect
c. Shadow Open Market Committee
d. Money creation

7. _____ is that which is owed; usually referencing assets owed, but the term can also cover moral obligations and other interactions not requiring money. In the case of assets, _____ is a means of using future purchasing power in the present before a summation has been earned. Some companies and corporations use _____ as a part of their overall corporate finance strategy.

a. Hard money loan
b. Debenture
c. Collateral Management
d. Debt

8. _____, in economics, is the quantity of money measured in a particular currency and is directly proportional to the price level.

This means, among other things, that if the price level rises by 10%, 10% more money than before is necessary in order to maintain stability. For example, if it costs $20 to buy an item, and the price level increases by 10%, the dollar amount necessary to buy the item increases by 10% (in this case by $2), which brings the total cost of the item to $22.

a. Limping bimetallism
b. Silver Thursday
c. Money of account
d. Nominal money

9. In economics, the _____ is a historical inverse relation between the rate of unemployment and the rate of inflation in an economy. Stated simply, the lower the unemployment in an economy, the higher the rate of increase in nominal wages in the economy. Rate of Change of Wages against Unemployment, United Kingdom 1913-1948 from Phillips (1958)

William Phillips, a New Zealand born economist, wrote a paper in 1958 titled The Relationship between Unemployment and the Rate of Change of Money Wages in the United Kingdom 1861-1957, which was published in the quarterly journal Economica.

a. Cost curve
b. Demand curve
c. Lorenz curve
d. Phillips curve

10. Bartering is a medium in which goods or services are directly exchanged for other goods and/or services, without the use of money. It can be bilateral or multilateral, and usually exists parallel to monetary systems in most developed countries, though to a very limited extent. _____ usually replaces money as the method of exchange in times of monetary crisis, when the currency is unstable and devalued by hyperinflation.

a. Community-based economics
b. Meitheal
c. Barter
d. New Economics Foundation

11. _____ occurs when the inhabitants of a country use foreign currency in parallel to or instead of the domestic currency.

_____ can occur

- unofficially, when private agents prefer the foreign currency over the domestic currency. They hold for example deposits in the foreign currency because of a bad track record of the local currency.

- semiofficially (or officially bimonetary systems), where foreign currency is legal tender, but plays a secondary role to domestic currency
- officially, when a country ceases to issue the domestic currency and uses only foreign currency. It adopts the foreign currency as legal tender.

The term _____ is not only applied to usage of the United States dollar, but also generally to the use of any foreign currency as the national currency.

 a. Commodity money   b. Currency board
 c. Dollarization   d. World currency

12. _____, 1st Baron Keynes was a renowned economist from Britain whose many ideas on economic and political theories as well as on many governments' monetary policies influenced America. He advocated a government that played an active role in the lives of people regarding business, economy, etc. In this role, the government would use fiscal measures to reduce the consequences of recessions, economic depressions and booms.
 a. Adam Smith   b. Adolf Hitler
 c. Adolph Fischer   d. John Maynard Keynes

13. _____ is a decrease in the rate of inflation. This phase of the business cycle, in which retailers can no longer pass on higher prices to their customers, often occurs during a recession. In contrast, deflation occurs when prices are actually dropping.
 a. Disinflation   b. Stealth inflation
 c. Reflation   d. Mundell-Tobin effect

14. In economics, _____ is the total demand for final goods and services in the economy (Y) at a given time and price level. It is the amount of goods and services in the economy that will be purchased at all possible price levels. This is the demand for the gross domestic product of a country when inventory levels are static.
 a. Aggregation problem   b. Aggregate supply
 c. Aggregate demand   d. Aggregate expenditure

15. Economics:

- _____, the desire to own something and the ability to pay for it
- _____ curve, a graphic representation of a _____ schedule
- _____ deposit, the money in checking accounts
- _____ pull theory, the theory that inflation occurs when _____ for goods and services exceeds existing supplies
- _____ schedule, a table that lists the quantity of a good a person will buy it each different price
- _____ side economics, the school of economics at believes government spending and tax cuts open economy by raising _____

a. Variability
b. McKesson ' Robbins scandal
c. Demand
d. Production

16. In economics, _____ is a rise in the general level of prices of goods and services in an economy over a period of time. When the general price level rises, each unit of currency buys fewer goods and services; consequently, _____ is also a decline in the real value of money--a loss of purchasing power in the medium of exchange which is also the monetary unit of account in the economy. A chief measure of general price-level _____ is the general _____ rate, which is the percentage change in a general price index (normally the Consumer Price Index) over time.

a. Economic
b. Opportunity cost
c. Inflation
d. Energy economics

17. In economics, the _____ is used to illustrate the idea that increases in the rate of taxation do not necessarily increase tax revenue. (For instance, whereas a 0% income tax rate will generate no revenue, neither will a 100% rate, as citizens will have no incentive to make money.) Increasing taxes beyond the peak of the curve point will decrease tax revenue.

a. 130-30 fund
b. 1921 recession
c. 100-year flood
d. Laffer curve

18. To _____ is to impose a financial charge or other levy upon a taxpayer by a state or the functional equivalent of a state.

_____ es are also imposed by many subnational entities. _____ es consist of direct _____ or indirect _____, and may be paid in money or as its labour equivalent (often but not always unpaid.)

a. 100-year flood
b. 1921 recession
c. 130-30 fund
d. Tax

19. To tax is to impose a financial charge or other levy upon a taxpayer by a state or the functional equivalent of a state.

_____ are also imposed by many subnational entities. _____ consist of direct tax or indirect tax, and may be paid in money or as its labour equivalent (often but not always unpaid.)

a. 1921 recession
b. 100-year flood
c. 130-30 fund
d. Taxes

Chapter 23. High Inflation

20. In calculus, a function f defined on a subset of the real numbers with real values is called _____, if for all x and y such that x >≤ y one has f(x) >≤ f(y), so f preserves the order. In layman's terms, the sign of the slope is always positive (the curve tending upwards) or zero (i.e., non-decreasing, or asymptotic, or depicted as a horizontal, flat line) Likewise, a function is called monotonically decreasing (non-increasing) if, whenever x >≤ y, then f(x) >≥ f(y), so it reverses the order.

- a. Monotonic
- b. 100-year flood
- c. 130-30 fund
- d. 1921 recession

21. _____ refers to the objective and subjective components of the believability of a source or message.

Traditionally, _____ has two key components: trustworthiness and expertise, which both have objective and subjective components. Trustworthiness is a based more on subjective factors, but can include objective measurements such as established reliability.

- a. 1921 recession
- b. 130-30 fund
- c. 100-year flood
- d. Credibility

22. _____ in economics are wage and price controls, most commonly instituted as a response to inflation, and usually below market level.

This type of policy dates to the Old Testament, in which Israelites were instructed not to charge interest to other Israelites. It was tried during the Roman Empire.

- a. Incomes policies
- b. Employment Cost Index
- c. Inflationary Spikes
- d. Inflation swap

23. The term _____ refers to government debt, expenditures and revenues, or to finance (particularly financial revenue) in general.

- _____ deficit is the budget deficit of federal or local government
- _____ policy is the discretionary spending of governments. Contrasts with monetary policy.
- _____ year and _____ quarter are reporting periods for firms and other agencies.

- a. Drawdown
- b. Fiscal
- c. Procter ' Gamble
- d. Bucket shop

Chapter 24. Should Policy Makers Be Restrained?

1. In economics, _____ is a rise in the general level of prices of goods and services in an economy over a period of time. When the general price level rises, each unit of currency buys fewer goods and services; consequently, _____ is also a decline in the real value of money--a loss of purchasing power in the medium of exchange which is also the monetary unit of account in the economy. A chief measure of general price-level _____ is the general _____ rate, which is the percentage change in a general price index (normally the Consumer Price Index) over time.
   a. Opportunity cost
   b. Energy economics
   c. Economic
   d. Inflation

2. In economics, the _____ is a measure of inflation, the rate of increase of a price index (for example, a consumer price index.)It is the percentage rate of change in price level over time. The rate of decrease in the purchasing power of money is approximately equal.

   It's used to calculate the real interest rate, as well as real increases in wages, and official measurements of this rate act as input variables to COLA adjustments and Inflation derivatives prices.

   a. Edgeworth paradox
   b. Inflation rate
   c. Interest rate option
   d. Equity value

3. A model in macroeconomics is a logical, mathematical, and/or computational framework designed to describe the operation of a national or regional economy, and especially the dynamics of aggregate quantities such as the total amount of goods and services produced, total income earned, the level of employment of productive resources, and the level of prices.

   There are different types of _____ that serve different purposes and have different advantages and disadvantages. Models are used to clarify and illustrate basic theoretical principles in macroeconomics; they are used to test, compare, and quantify different theories of the macroeconomy; they are used to produce 'what if' scenarios, and especially to evaluate the possible effects of changes in monetary, fiscal, or other macroeconomic policies; and they are used for generating economic forecasts.

   a. High-powered money
   b. Factor shares
   c. Macroeconomic models
   d. Natural rate of unemployment

4. The _____ is an economic and political union of 27 member states, located primarily in Europe. It was established by the Treaty of Maastricht on 1 November 1993, upon the foundations of the pre-existing European Economic Community. With a population of almost 500 million, the _____ generates an estimated 30% share (US$18.4 trillion in 2008) of the nominal gross world product.
   a. ACCRA Cost of Living Index
   b. European Court of Justice
   c. ACEA agreement
   d. European Union

5. _____ is a branch of applied mathematics that is used in the social sciences (most notably economics), biology, engineering, political science, international relations, computer science, and philosophy. _____ attempts to mathematically capture behavior in strategic situations, in which an individual's success in making choices depends on the choices of others. While initially developed to analyze competitions in which one individual does better at another's expense (zero sum games), it has been expanded to treat a wide class of interactions, which are classified according to several criteria.
   a. Proper equilibrium
   b. Discriminatory price auction
   c. Dollar auction
   d. Game theory

Chapter 24. Should Policy Makers Be Restrained?

6. In economics, the _____ is a historical inverse relation between the rate of unemployment and the rate of inflation in an economy. Stated simply, the lower the unemployment in an economy, the higher the rate of increase in nominal wages in the economy. Rate of Change of Wages against Unemployment, United Kingdom 1913-1948 from Phillips (1958)

William Phillips, a New Zealand born economist, wrote a paper in 1958 titled The Relationship between Unemployment and the Rate of Change of Money Wages in the United Kingdom 1861-1957, which was published in the quarterly journal Economica.

   a. Demand curve
   b. Cost curve
   c. Lorenz curve
   d. Phillips curve

7. In economics, _____ describes a situation where a decision-maker's preferences change over time, such that what is preferred at one point in time is inconsistent with what is preferred at another point in time. It is often easiest to think about preferences over time in this context by thinking of decision-makers as being made up of many different 'selves', with each self representing the decision-maker at a different point in time. So, for example, there is my today self, my tomorrow self, my next Tuesday self, my year from now self, etc.
   a. Dynamic inconsistency
   b. Cheap talk
   c. Graph continuous
   d. Bondareva-Shapley theorem

8. A _____, reserve bank, or monetary authority is the entity responsible for the monetary policy of a country or of a group of member states. It is a bank that can lend money to other banks in times of need. Its primary responsibility is to maintain the stability of the national currency and money supply, but more active duties include controlling subsidized-loan interest rates, and acting as a lender of last resort to the banking sector during times of financial crisis (private banks often being integral to the national financial system.)
   a. 100-year flood
   b. 130-30 fund
   c. 1921 recession
   d. Central bank

9. _____ refers to the objective and subjective components of the believability of a source or message.

Traditionally, _____ has two key components: trustworthiness and expertise, which both have objective and subjective components. Trustworthiness is a based more on subjective factors, but can include objective measurements such as established reliability.

   a. 1921 recession
   b. Credibility
   c. 100-year flood
   d. 130-30 fund

10. A _____ proof is a mathematical proof that a particular theory is consistent. The early development of mathematical proof theory was driven by the desire to provide finitary _____ proofs for all of mathematics as part of Hilbert's program. Hilbert's program was strongly impacted by incompleteness theorems, which showed that sufficiently strong proof theories cannot prove their own _____
   a. 130-30 fund
   b. 100-year flood
   c. Consistency
   d. Reason

Chapter 24. Should Policy Makers Be Restrained?

11. The term _____ refers to economy-wide fluctuations in production or economic activity over several months or years. These fluctuations occur around a long-term growth trend, and typically involve shifts over time between periods of relatively rapid economic growth (expansion or boom), and periods of relative stagnation or decline (contraction or recession.)

These fluctuations are often measured using the growth rate of real gross domestic product.

a. Tobit model
c. Business cycle
b. Consumer theory
d. Nominal value

12. The _____ is the official currency of 16 of the 27 member states of the European Union (EU.) The states, known collectively as the Eurozone, are Austria, Belgium, Cyprus, Finland, France, Germany, Greece, Ireland, Italy, Luxembourg, Malta, the Netherlands, Portugal, Slovakia, Slovenia, and Spain. The currency is also used in a further five European countries, with and without formal agreements and is consequently used daily by some 327 million Europeans.

a. Import and Export Price Indices
c. IRS Code 3401
b. Equity capital market
d. Euro

13. The _____ was signed on 7 February 1992 in Maastricht, the Netherlands after final negotiations on 9 December 1991 between the members of the European Community and entered into force on 1 November 1993 during the Delors Commission. It created the European Union and led to the creation of the euro. The _____ has been amended to a degree by later treaties.

a. 100-year flood
c. Treaties of Rome
b. Treaty of Amsterdam
d. Maastricht Treaty

14. The term _____ refers to government debt, expenditures and revenues, or to finance (particularly financial revenue) in general.

- _____ deficit is the budget deficit of federal or local government
- _____ policy is the discretionary spending of governments. Contrasts with monetary policy.
- _____ year and _____ quarter are reporting periods for firms and other agencies.

a. Bucket shop
c. Drawdown
b. Fiscal
d. Procter ' Gamble

15. In economics, _____ is the use of government spending and revenue collection to influence the economy.

_____ can be contrasted with the other main type of economic policy, monetary policy, which attempts to stabilize the economy by controlling interest rates and the supply of money. The two main instruments of _____ are government spending and taxation.

a. Fiscalism
c. Fiscal policy
b. Sustainable investment rule
d. 100-year flood

16. _____ is a common concept in economics, and gives rise to derived concepts such as consumer debt. Generally _____ is defined by opposition to production. But the precise definition can vary because different schools of economists define production quite differently.

   a. Federal Reserve Bank Notes   b. Consumption
   c. Foreclosure data providers   d. Cash or share options

17. From a Keynesian point of view, a _____ in the public sector is achieved when the government equates the revenues with expenditure over the business cycles. In other words, a government's budget is balanced if its income is equal to its expenditure. It is a budget in which revenues are equal to spending.

   a. Budget theory   b. Balanced budget
   c. Budget crisis   d. Budget support

Chapter 24. Should Policy Makers Be Restrained?

18. A _____ is:

   - Rewrite _____, in generative grammar and computer science
   - Standardization, a formal and widely-accepted statement, fact, definition, or qualification
   - Operation, a determinate _____ for performing a mathematical operation and obtaining a certain result (Mathematics, Logic)
     - Unary operation
     - Binary operation
   - _____ of inference, a function from sets of formulae to formulae (Mathematics, Logic)
   - _____ of thumb, principle with broad application that is not intended to be strictly accurate or reliable for every situation. Also often simply referred to as a _____
   - Moral, an atomic element of a moral code for guiding choices in human behavior
   - Heuristic, a quantized '_____' which shows a tendency or probability for successful function
   - A regulation, as in sports
   - A Production _____, as in computer science
   - Procedural law, a _____ set governing the application of laws to cases
     - A law, which may informally be called a '_____'
     - A court ruling, a decision by a court
   - In the U.S. Government, a regulation mandated by Congress, but written or expanded upon by the Executive Branch.
   - Norm (sociology), an informal but widely accepted _____, concept, truth, definition, or qualification (social norms, legal norms, coding norms)
   - Norm (philosophy), a kind of sentence or a reason to act, feel or believe
   - 'Rulership' is the concept of governance by a government:
     - Military _____, governance by a military body
     - Monastic _____, a collection of precepts that guides the life of monks or nuns in a religious order where the superior holds the place of Christ
   - Slide _____

   - '_____,' a song by Ayumi Hamasaki
   - '_____,' a song by rapper Nas
   - '_____s,' an album by the band The Whitest Boy Alive
   - _____s: Pyaar Ka Superhit Formula, a 2003 Bollywood film
   - ruler, an instrument for measuring lengths
   - _____, a component of an astrolabe, circumferator or similar instrument
   - The _____s, a bestselling self-help book
   - _____ Project (Run Up-to-date Linux Everywhere), a project that aims to use up-to-date Linux software on old PCs
   - _____ engine, a software system that helps managing business _____s
   - Ja _____, a hip hop artist
     - R.U.L.E., a 2005 greatest hits album by rapper Ja _____
   - '_____s,' a KMFDM song

a. Procter ' Gamble   b. Demand
c. Technocracy   d. Rule

Chapter 25. Monetary Policy: A Summing Up

1. _____s is the social science that studies the production, distribution, and consumption of goods and services. The term _____s comes from the Ancient Greek οá¼°κονομῖα from οá¼¶κος (oikos, 'house') + vĩŒµος (nomos, 'custom' or 'law'), hence 'rules of the house(hold)'. Current _____ models developed out of the broader field of political economy in the late 19th century, owing to a desire to use an empirical approach more akin to the physical sciences.
   a. Economic
   b. Opportunity cost
   c. Energy economics
   d. Inflation

2. In economics, _____ is a rise in the general level of prices of goods and services in an economy over a period of time. When the general price level rises, each unit of currency buys fewer goods and services; consequently, _____ is also a decline in the real value of money--a loss of purchasing power in the medium of exchange which is also the monetary unit of account in the economy. A chief measure of general price-level _____ is the general _____ rate, which is the percentage change in a general price index (normally the Consumer Price Index) over time.
   a. Opportunity cost
   b. Energy economics
   c. Economic
   d. Inflation

3. In economics, the _____ is a measure of inflation, the rate of increase of a price index (for example, a consumer price index.)It is the percentage rate of change in price level over time. The rate of decrease in the purchasing power of money is approximately equal.

   It's used to calculate the real interest rate, as well as real increases in wages, and official measurements of this rate act as input variables to COLA adjustments and Inflation derivatives prices.

   a. Interest rate option
   b. Equity value
   c. Edgeworth paradox
   d. Inflation rate

4. _____ is a decrease in the rate of inflation. This phase of the business cycle, in which retailers can no longer pass on higher prices to their customers, often occurs during a recession. In contrast, deflation occurs when prices are actually dropping.
   a. Disinflation
   b. Reflation
   c. Stealth inflation
   d. Mundell-Tobin effect

5. In economics, _____ is inflation that is very high or 'out of control', a condition in which prices increase rapidly as a currency loses its value. Definitions used by the media vary from a cumulative inflation rate over three years approaching 100% to 'inflation exceeding 50% a month.' In informal usage the term is often applied to much lower rates. As a rule of thumb, normal inflation is reported per year, but _____ is often reported for much shorter intervals, often per month.
   a. 100-year flood
   b. Hyperinflation
   c. 1921 recession
   d. 130-30 fund

6. To _____ is to impose a financial charge or other levy upon a taxpayer by a state or the functional equivalent of a state.

   _____es are also imposed by many subnational entities. _____es consist of direct _____ or indirect _____, and may be paid in money or as its labour equivalent (often but not always unpaid.)

   a. 1921 recession
   b. 130-30 fund
   c. 100-year flood
   d. Tax

7. In economics, _____ refers to the tendency of people to think of currency in nominal, rather than real, terms. In other words, the numerical/face value (nominal value) of money is mistaken for its purchasing power (real value.) This is a fallacy as modern fiat currencies have no inherent value and their real value is derived from their ability to be exchanged for goods and used for payment of taxes.

   a. Representative money   b. Money changer
   c. Metallism   d. Money illusion

8. In economics, the _____ is a historical inverse relation between the rate of unemployment and the rate of inflation in an economy. Stated simply, the lower the unemployment in an economy, the higher the rate of increase in nominal wages in the economy. Rate of Change of Wages against Unemployment, United Kingdom 1913-1948 from Phillips (1958)

William Phillips, a New Zealand born economist, wrote a paper in 1958 titled The Relationship between Unemployment and the Rate of Change of Money Wages in the United Kingdom 1861-1957, which was published in the quarterly journal Economica.

   a. Demand curve   b. Cost curve
   c. Lorenz curve   d. Phillips curve

9. The term _____, 'the state or characteristic of being variable', _____ describes how spread out or closely clustered a set of data is. may be applied to many different subjects:

- Climate _____
- Genetic _____
- Heart rate _____
- Human _____
- Solar van
- Spatial _____
- Statistical _____
- _____

   a. Variability   b. Total product
   c. Characteristic   d. Demand

10. A _____, reserve bank, or monetary authority is the entity responsible for the monetary policy of a country or of a group of member states. It is a bank that can lend money to other banks in times of need. Its primary responsibility is to maintain the stability of the national currency and money supply, but more active duties include controlling subsidized-loan interest rates, and acting as a lender of last resort to the banking sector during times of financial crisis (private banks often being integral to the national financial system.)

   a. Central bank   b. 1921 recession
   c. 100-year flood   d. 130-30 fund

11. _____ is the process by which the government, central bank (ii) availability of money, and (iii) cost of money or rate of interest, in order to attain a set of objectives oriented towards the growth and stability of the economy. Monetary theory provides insight into how to craft optimal _____.

_____ is referred to as either being an expansionary policy where an expansionary policy increases the total supply of money in the economy, and a contractionary policy decreases the total money supply.

a. 130-30 fund
b. 100-year flood
c. 1921 recession
d. Monetary policy

12. In finance, a _____ is a debt security, in which the authorized issuer owes the holders a debt and, depending on the terms of the _____, is obliged to pay interest (the coupon) and/or to repay the principal at a later date, termed maturity. A _____ is a formal contract to repay borrowed money with interest at fixed intervals.

Thus a _____ is like a loan: the issuer is the borrower (debtor), the holder is the lender (creditor), and the coupon is the interest.

a. Bond
b. Prize Bond
c. Zero-coupon
d. Callable

13. _____ refers to the objective and subjective components of the believability of a source or message.

Traditionally, _____ has two key components: trustworthiness and expertise, which both have objective and subjective components. Trustworthiness is a based more on subjective factors, but can include objective measurements such as established reliability.

a. 100-year flood
b. Credibility
c. 1921 recession
d. 130-30 fund

14. In economics, _____ is the widest measurement of the money supply. It is generally

'One measure of the money supply that includes M1, plus savings and small time deposits, overnight repos at commercial banks, and non-institutional money market accounts. This is a key economic indicator used to forecast inflation, since it is not as narrow as M1 and still relatively easy to track.

a. Club goods
b. Buy-side analyst
c. Flight-to-quality
d. Broad money

15. In business and accounting, _____ are everything of value that is owned by a person or company. It is a claim on the property your income of a borrower. The balance sheet of a firm records the monetary value of the _____ owned by the firm.

a. ACEA agreement
b. ACCRA Cost of Living Index
c. Amortization schedule
d. Assets

16. In economics, a _____ is a monetary-policy rule that stipulates how much the central bank would or should change the nominal interest rate in response to divergences of actual inflation rates from target inflation rates and of actual Gross Domestic Product (GDP) from potential GDP. It was first proposed by the by U.S. economist John B. Taylor in 1993. The rule can be written as follows:

$$i_t = \pi_t + r_t^* + a_\pi(\pi_t - \pi_t^*) + a_y(y_t - \bar{y}_t).$$

In this equation, i_t is the target short-term nominal interest rate (e.g. the federal funds rate in the US), π_t is the rate of inflation as measured by the GDP deflator, π_t^* is the desired rate of inflation, r_t^* is the assumed equilibrium real interest rate, y_t is the logarithm of real GDP, and $\bar{y}_t$ is the logarithm of potential output, as determined by a linear trend.

a. Term Securities Lending Facility
c. Federal Reserve Banks
b. Fed Funds Probability
d. Taylor rule

Chapter 25. Monetary Policy: A Summing Up

17. A _____ is:

   - Rewrite _____, in generative grammar and computer science
   - Standardization, a formal and widely-accepted statement, fact, definition, or qualification
   - Operation, a determinate _____ for performing a mathematical operation and obtaining a certain result (Mathematics, Logic)
       - Unary operation
       - Binary operation
   - _____ of inference, a function from sets of formulae to formulae (Mathematics, Logic)
   - _____ of thumb, principle with broad application that is not intended to be strictly accurate or reliable for every situation. Also often simply referred to as a _____
   - Moral, an atomic element of a moral code for guiding choices in human behavior
   - Heuristic, a quantized '_____' which shows a tendency or probability for successful function
   - A regulation, as in sports
   - A Production _____, as in computer science
   - Procedural law, a _____ set governing the application of laws to cases
       - A law, which may informally be called a '_____'
       - A court ruling, a decision by a court
   - In the U.S. Government, a regulation mandated by Congress, but written or expanded upon by the Executive Branch.
   - Norm (sociology), an informal but widely accepted _____, concept, truth, definition, or qualification (social norms, legal norms, coding norms)
   - Norm (philosophy), a kind of sentence or a reason to act, feel or believe
   - 'Rulership' is the concept of governance by a government:
       - Military _____, governance by a military body
       - Monastic _____, a collection of precepts that guides the life of monks or nuns in a religious order where the superior holds the place of Christ
   - Slide _____

   - '_____,' a song by Ayumi Hamasaki
   - '_____,' a song by rapper Nas
   - '_____s,' an album by the band The Whitest Boy Alive
   - _____s: Pyaar Ka Superhit Formula, a 2003 Bollywood film
   - ruler, an instrument for measuring lengths
   - _____, a component of an astrolabe, circumferator or similar instrument
   - The _____s, a bestselling self-help book
   - _____ Project (Run Up-to-date Linux Everywhere), a project that aims to use up-to-date Linux software on old PCs
   - _____ engine, a software system that helps managing business _____s
   - Ja _____, a hip hop artist
       - R.U.L.E., a 2005 greatest hits album by rapper Ja _____
   - '_____s,' a KMFDM song

a. Technocracy
c. Demand
b. Procter ' Gamble
d. Rule

18. _____s are a type of administrative division, in some countries managed by a local government. They vary greatly in size, spanning entire regions or counties, several municipalities, or subdivisions of municipalities.

In Austria, a _____ or Bezirk is an administrative division normally encompassing several municipalities, roughly equivalent to the Landkreis in Germany.

a. District
b. 130-30 fund
c. 100-year flood
d. 1921 recession

19. The _____ , a component of the Federal Reserve System, is charged under United States law with overseeing the nation's open market operations. It is the Federal Reserve Committee that makes key decisions about interest rates and the growth jam of the United States money supply. It is the principal organ of United States national monetary policy.

a. Fed Funds Probability
b. Primary Dealer Credit Facility
c. Federal Open Market Committee
d. Federal Reserve Transparency Act

20. In the United States, the _____ also known as the Federal Reserve Banks are the twelve banking districts created by the Federal Reserve Act.

The twelve _____

The _____ are as follows:

1. Boston
2. New York
3. Philadelphia
4. Cleveland
5. Richmond
6. Atlanta
7. Chicago
8. St Louis
9. Minneapolis
10. Kansas City
11. Dallas
12. San Francisco

a. Free contract
b. Lean consumption
c. Federal Reserve Districts
d. Residual claimant

21. In economics, the _____ is the term used to refer to the environment in which bonds are bought and sold between a central bank ' its regulated banks. It is not a free market process.

- To intervene in the 'business cycle', a central bank may choose to go into the _____ and buy or sell government bonds, which is known as _____ operations to increase reserves.

Chapter 25. Monetary Policy: A Summing Up

a. Inside money
b. Outside money
c. ACCRA Cost of Living Index
d. Open Market

22. Discounting is a financial mechanism in which a debtor obtains the right to delay payments to a creditor, for a defined period of time, in exchange for a charge or fee. Essentially, the party that owes money in the present purchases the right to delay the payment until some future date. The _____, or charge, is simply the difference between the original amount owed in the present and the amount that has to be paid in the future to settle the debt.

a. Certified Risk Manager
b. Discount
c. Reliability theory
d. Reinsurance

23. The _____ is an interest rate a central bank charges depository institutions that borrow reserves from it.

The term _____ has two meanings:

- the same as interest rate; the term 'discount' does not refer to the meaning of the word, but to the purpose of using the quantity, such as computations of present value, e.g. net present value or discounted cash flow

- the annual effective _____, which is the annual interest divided by the capital including that interest; this rate is lower than the interest rate; it corresponds to using the value after a year as the nominal value, and seeing the initial value as the nominal value minus a discount; it is used for Treasury Bills and similar financial instruments

The annual effective _____ is the annual interest divided by the capital including that interest, which is the interest rate divided by 100% plus the interest rate. It is the annual discount factor to be applied to the future cash flow, to find the discount, subtracted from a future value to find the value one year earlier.

For example, suppose there is a government bond that sells for $95 and pays $100 in a year's time.

a. Discount rate
b. Stochastic volatility
c. Johansen test
d. Perpetuity

24. The _____ is an instrument of monetary policy (usually controlled by central banks) that allows eligible institutions to borrow money from the central bank, usually on a short-term basis, to meet temporary shortages of liquidity caused by internal or external disruptions. The term originated with the practice of sending a bank representative to a reserve bank teller window when a bank needed to borrow money.

The interest rate charged on such loans by a central bank is called the discount rate, base rate, repo rate, or primary rate.

a. Private money
b. Discount window
c. Prime rate
d. Capital requirement

25. The _____ is a bank regulation that sets the minimum reserves each bank must hold to customer deposits and notes. It would normally be in the form of fiat currency stored in a bank vault (vault cash), or with a central bank.

Chapter 25. Monetary Policy: A Summing Up

The reserve ratio is sometimes used as a tool in the monetary policy, influencing the country's economy, borrowing, and interest rates.

a. Reserve requirement
b. Fractional-reserve banking
c. Probability of default
d. Private money

26. In the United States, _____ are overnight borrowings by banks to maintain their bank reserves at the Federal Reserve. Banks keep reserves at Federal Reserve Banks to meet their reserve requirements and to clear financial transactions. Transactions in the _____ market enable depository institutions with reserve balances in excess of reserve requirements to lend reserves to institutions with reserve deficiencies.

a. Term auction facility
b. Federal funds rate
c. Federal Reserve Transparency Act
d. Federal funds

27. In the United States, the _____ is the interest rate at which private depository institutions (mostly banks) lend balances (federal funds) at the Federal Reserve to other depository institutions, usually overnight. It is the interest rate banks charge each other for loans. Changing the target rate is one way the Chairman of the Federal Reserve can influence the supply of money in the U.S. economy..

a. Federal banking
b. Federal funds rate
c. Monetary Policy Report to the Congress
d. Term auction facility

28. In economics, a _____ is a mechanism that allows people to easily buy and sell (trade) financial securities (such as stocks and bonds), commodities (such as precious metals or agricultural goods), and other fungible items of value at low transaction costs and at prices that reflect the efficient-market hypothesis.

_____s have evolved significantly over several hundred years and are undergoing constant innovation to improve liquidity.

Both general markets (where many commodities are traded) and specialized markets (where only one commodity is traded) exist.

a. Convertible arbitrage
b. Noise trader
c. Market anomaly
d. Financial market

29. _____ is an American economist and was the Chairman of the Federal Reserve of the United States from 1987 to 2006. He currently works as a private advisor and providing consulting for firms through his company, Greenspan Associates LLC.

First appointed Federal Reserve chairman by President Ronald Reagan in August 1987, he was reappointed at successive four-year intervals until retiring on January 31, 2006 after the second-longest tenure in the position.

a. Adam Smith
b. Alan Greenspan
c. Adolph Fischer
d. Adolf Hitler

30. In economics, the _____ measures the payments that flow between any individual country and all other countries. It is used to summarize all international economic transactions for that country during a specific time period, usually a year. The _____ is determined by the country's exports and imports of goods, services, and financial capital, as well as financial transfers.

   a. Gross world product
   b. Skyscraper Index
   c. Gross domestic product per barrel
   d. Balance of payments

31. A _____ is the transfer of wealth from one party (such as a person or company) to another. A _____ is usually made in exchange for the provision of goods, services or both, or to fulfill a legal obligation.

The simplest and oldest form of _____ is barter, the exchange of one good or service for another.

   a. Soft count
   b. Payment
   c. Going concern
   d. Social gravity

Chapter 26. Fiscal Policy: A Summing Up

1. _____ is that which is owed; usually referencing assets owed, but the term can also cover moral obligations and other interactions not requiring money. In the case of assets, _____ is a means of using future purchasing power in the present before a summation has been earned. Some companies and corporations use _____ as a part of their overall corporate finance strategy.
   a. Debenture
   b. Collateral Management
   c. Hard money loan
   d. Debt

2. A _____ is a legal document that is often passed by the legislature, and approved by the chief executive-or president. For example, only certain types of revenue may be imposed and collected. Property tax is frequently the basis for municipal and county revenues, while sales tax and/or income tax are the basis for state revenues, and income tax and corporate tax are the basis for national revenues.
   a. Lump-sum tax
   b. Right-financing
   c. Government budget
   d. Structural deficit

3. A _____ represents the combinations of goods and services that a consumer can purchase given current prices and his income. Consumer theory uses the concepts of a _____ and a preference map to analyze consumer choices. Both concepts have a ready graphical representation in the two-good case.
   a. Quality bias
   b. Revealed preference
   c. Joint demand
   d. Budget constraint

4. _____ is the pure deficit which is derived after deducting the interest payments component from the total deficit of any budget.

   In other words the total of _____ and interest payments makes the fiscal deficit.

   The opposite of a _____ is a primary surplus.

   a. Standard of deferred payment
   b. Bond credit rating
   c. Revolving account
   d. Primary deficit

5. _____ is a decrease in the rate of inflation. This phase of the business cycle, in which retailers can no longer pass on higher prices to their customers, often occurs during a recession. In contrast, deflation occurs when prices are actually dropping.
   a. Reflation
   b. Disinflation
   c. Stealth inflation
   d. Mundell-Tobin effect

6. In economics, _____ is inflation that is very high or 'out of control', a condition in which prices increase rapidly as a currency loses its value. Definitions used by the media vary from a cumulative inflation rate over three years approaching 100% to 'inflation exceeding 50% a month.' In informal usage the term is often applied to much lower rates. As a rule of thumb, normal inflation is reported per year, but _____ is often reported for much shorter intervals, often per month.
   a. 1921 recession
   b. Hyperinflation
   c. 100-year flood
   d. 130-30 fund

7. To _____ is to impose a financial charge or other levy upon a taxpayer by a state or the functional equivalent of a state.

_____es are also imposed by many subnational entities. _____es consist of direct _____ or indirect _____, and may be paid in money or as its labour equivalent (often but not always unpaid.)

a. 1921 recession
c. 130-30 fund
b. 100-year flood
d. Tax

8. To tax is to impose a financial charge or other levy upon a taxpayer by a state or the functional equivalent of a state.

_____ are also imposed by many subnational entities. _____ consist of direct tax or indirect tax, and may be paid in money or as its labour equivalent (often but not always unpaid.)

a. 1921 recession
c. 100-year flood
b. 130-30 fund
d. Taxes

9. _____ is a financial ratio that indicates the percentage of a company's assets are provided via debt. It is the ratio of total debt (the sum of current liabilities and long-term liabilities) and total assets (the sum of current assets, fixed assets, and other assets such as 'goodwill'.)

$$\text{Debt ratio} = \frac{\text{Total Debt}}{\text{Total Assets}}$$

or alternatively:

$$\text{Debt ratio} = \frac{\text{Total Liability}}{\text{Total Assets}}$$

For example, a company with $2 million in total assets and $500,000 in total liabilities would have a _____ of 25%

Like all financial ratios, a company's _____ should be compared with their industry average or other competing firms.

a. Chinese wall
c. Debt ratio
b. Cash management
d. Customer Demand Planning

10. A _____ is an expression that compares quantities relative to each other. The most common examples involve two quantities, but any number of quantities can be compared. _____s are represented mathematically by separating each quantity with a colon, for example the _____ 2:3, which is read as the _____ 'two to three'.

a. Ratio
c. Y-intercept
b. 100-year flood
d. 130-30 fund

11. _____s is the social science that studies the production, distribution, and consumption of goods and services. The term _____s comes from the Ancient Greek oá¼°κονομῖα from oá¼¶κος (oikos, 'house') + νΌεμος (nomos, 'custom' or 'law'), hence 'rules of the house(hold)'. Current _____ models developed out of the broader field of political economy in the late 19th century, owing to a desire to use an empirical approach more akin to the physical sciences.

a. Economic
b. Energy economics
c. Inflation
d. Opportunity cost

12. _____, is an economic theory that suggests consumers internalise the government's budget constraint and thus the timing of any tax change does not affect their change in spending. Consequently, _____ suggests that it does not matter whether a government finances its spending with debt or a tax increase, the effect on total level of demand in an economy will be the same. It was proposed, and then rejected, by the 19th-century economist David Ricardo.

a. Social discount rate
b. Municipalization
c. Quasi-market
d. Ricardian equivalence

13. The term _____ refers to government debt, expenditures and revenues, or to finance (particularly financial revenue) in general.

- _____ deficit is the budget deficit of federal or local government
- _____ policy is the discretionary spending of governments. Contrasts with monetary policy.
- _____ year and _____ quarter are reporting periods for firms and other agencies.

a. Bucket shop
b. Drawdown
c. Procter ' Gamble
d. Fiscal

14. In economics, _____ is the use of government spending and revenue collection to influence the economy.

_____ can be contrasted with the other main type of economic policy, monetary policy, which attempts to stabilize the economy by controlling interest rates and the supply of money. The two main instruments of _____ are government spending and taxation.

a. Fiscalism
b. Fiscal policy
c. Sustainable investment rule
d. 100-year flood

15. _____ forms part of the public sector deficit. _____ differs from cyclical deficit in that it exists even when the economy is at its potential.

_____ issues can only be addressed by explicit and direct government policies: reducing spending (including entitlements), increasing the tax base, and/or increasing tax rates.

a. Sovereign credit
b. Tax increment financing
c. Minimum Municipal Obligation
d. Structural deficit

16. A _____ is a situation in which the government takes in more than it spends.

a. Budget set
b. 130-30 fund
c. Budget surplus
d. 100-year flood

17. In statistics and image processing, to smooth a data set is to create an approximating function that attempts to capture important patterns in the data, while leaving out noise or other fine-scale structures/rapid phenomena. Many different algorithms are used in _____. One of the most common algorithms is the 'moving average', often used to try to capture important trends in repeated statistical surveys.

a. Partial regression plot
b. X-bar chart
c. Partial residual plot
d. Smoothing

18. _____ is a common concept in economics, and gives rise to derived concepts such as consumer debt. Generally _____ is defined by opposition to production. But the precise definition can vary because different schools of economists define production quite differently.

a. Consumption
b. Foreclosure data providers
c. Federal Reserve Bank Notes
d. Cash or share options

19. A variety of measures of _____ and output are used in economics to estimate total economic activity in a country or region, including gross domestic product (GDP), gross national product (GNP), and net _____.

There are three main ways of calculating these numbers; the output approach, the income approach and the expenditure approach. In theory, the three must yield the same, because total expenditures on goods and services must equal the total income paid to the producers (Gnational income), and that must also equal the total value of the output of goods and services (GNP.)

a. Volume index
b. GNI per capita
c. Gross world product
d. National Income

20. _____ use double-entry accounting to report the monetary value and sources of output produced in a country and the distribution of incomes that production generates. Data are available at the national and industry levels.

The NIPA summarizes national income on the left (debit, revenue) side and national product on the right (credit, expense) side of a two-column accounting report.

a. National Income and Product Accounts
b. Current account
c. Gross private domestic investment
d. Net national product

21. A _____ is a reduction in taxes. Economic stimulus via _____s, along with interest rate intervention and deficit spending, are one of the central tenets of Keynesian economics.

The immediate effects of a _____ are, generally, a decrease in the real income of the government and an increase in the real income of those whose tax rate has been lowered.

a. Withholding tax
b. Direct taxes
c. Popiwek
d. Tax cut

22. _____ is the point where a person stops employment completely. A person may also semi-retire and keep some sort of _____ job, out of choice rather than necessity. This usually happens upon reaching a determined age, when physical conditions don't allow the person to work any more (by illness or accident), or even for personal choice (usually in the presence of an adequate pension or personal savings.)

a. Termination of employment
b. 100-year flood
c. Layoff
d. Retirement

Chapter 27. Epilogue: The Story of Macroeconomics

1. In economics, _____ is the total demand for final goods and services in the economy (Y) at a given time and price level. It is the amount of goods and services in the economy that will be purchased at all possible price levels. This is the demand for the gross domestic product of a country when inventory levels are static.

   a. Aggregate supply
   b. Aggregate expenditure
   c. Aggregation problem
   d. Aggregate demand

2. The term _____ refers to economy-wide fluctuations in production or economic activity over several months or years. These fluctuations occur around a long-term growth trend, and typically involve shifts over time between periods of relatively rapid economic growth (expansion or boom), and periods of relative stagnation or decline (contraction or recession.)

   These fluctuations are often measured using the growth rate of real gross domestic product.

   a. Consumer theory
   b. Nominal value
   c. Tobit model
   d. Business cycle

3. Economics:

   - _____, the desire to own something and the ability to pay for it
   - _____ curve, a graphic representation of a _____ schedule
   - _____ deposit, the money in checking accounts
   - _____ pull theory, the theory that inflation occurs when _____ for goods and services exceeds existing supplies
   - _____ schedule, a table that lists the quantity of a good a person will buy it each different price
   - _____ side economics, the school of economics at believes government spending and tax cuts open economy by raising _____

   a. McKesson ' Robbins scandal
   b. Production
   c. Variability
   d. Demand

4. _____ , is an economic principle that suggests consumer needs and desires must be accompanied by purchasing power (money) to be considered effective in discussions of supply and demand for the determination of price.

   Classical economists Adam Smith and David Ricardo embraced Say's Law, suggesting that 'supply creates its own demand.' According to Say's Law, for every excess supply (glut) of goods in one market, there is a corresponding excess demand (shortage) in another. This theory suggests that a general glut can never be accompanied by inadequate demand for products on a macroeconomic level.

   a. Effective demand
   b. AD-IA Model
   c. ACCRA Cost of Living Index
   d. ACEA agreement

5. _____ is a fee paid on borrowed assets. It is the price paid for the use of borrowed money, or, money earned by deposited funds. Assets that are sometimes lent with _____ include money, shares, consumer goods through hire purchase, major assets such as aircraft, and even entire factories in finance lease arrangements.

a. Internal debt
b. Insolvency
c. Asset protection
d. Interest

6. _____, 1st Baron Keynes was a renowned economist from Britain whose many ideas on economic and political theories as well as on many governments' monetary policies influenced America. He advocated a government that played an active role in the lives of people regarding business, economy, etc. In this role, the government would use fiscal measures to reduce the consequences of recessions, economic depressions and booms.
a. Adam Smith
b. Adolf Hitler
c. Adolph Fischer
d. John Maynard Keynes

7. Market _____ is a business, economics or investment term that refers to an asset's ability to be easily converted through an act of buying or selling without causing a significant movement in the price and with minimum loss of value. Money, or cash on hand, is the most liquid asset. An act of exchange of a less liquid asset with a more liquid asset is called liquidation.
a. 100-year flood
b. 130-30 fund
c. 1921 recession
d. Liquidity

8. _____ in macroeconomic theory refers to the demand for money, considered as liquidity. The concept was first developed by John Maynard Keynes in his book The General Theory of Employment, Interest and Money (1936) to explain determination of the interest rate by the supply and demand for money. The demand for money as an asset was theorized to depend on the interest foregone by not holding bonds.
a. Liquidity preference
b. DAD-SAS model
c. Consumption function
d. Forward premium anomaly

9. _____ was a postwar academic movement in economics that attempted to absorb the macroeconomic thought of John Maynard Keynes into the thought of neoclassical economics. Mainstream economics is largely dominated by the synthesis, being largely Keynesian on macroeconomics and neoclassical on microeconomics.

The theory was developed by John Hicks, and popularized by the mathematical economist Paul Samuelson, who seems to have coined the term, and helped disseminate the 'synthesis,' partly through his technical writing and in his influential textbook, Economics.

a. Reaganomics
b. Growth accounting
c. Great divergence
d. Neoclassical synthesis

10. A _____, reserve bank, or monetary authority is the entity responsible for the monetary policy of a country or of a group of member states. It is a bank that can lend money to other banks in times of need. Its primary responsibility is to maintain the stability of the national currency and money supply, but more active duties include controlling subsidized-loan interest rates, and acting as a lender of last resort to the banking sector during times of financial crisis (private banks often being integral to the national financial system.)
a. Central bank
b. 100-year flood
c. 130-30 fund
d. 1921 recession

11. _____ is a common concept in economics, and gives rise to derived concepts such as consumer debt. Generally _____ is defined by opposition to production. But the precise definition can vary because different schools of economists define production quite differently.

a. Foreclosure data providers
b. Consumption
c. Cash or share options
d. Federal Reserve Bank Notes

12. _____ was an American economist, statistician and public intellectual, and a recipient of the Nobel Memorial Prize in Economic Sciences. He is best known among scholars for his theoretical and empirical research, especially consumption analysis, monetary history and theory, and for his demonstration of the complexity of stabilization policy. A global public followed his restatement of a political philosophy that insisted on minimizing the role of government in favor of the private sector.
   a. Adam Smith
   b. Adolf Hitler
   c. Adolph Fischer
   d. Milton Friedman

13. _____ encompasses the body of knowledge used to support the decision-making process of choosing investments for various purposes. It includes portfolio theory, the Capital Asset Pricing Model, Arbitrage Pricing Theory, and the Efficient market hypothesis.
   a. Alternative investment
   b. Investment theory
   c. Over-investing
   d. Asset price crash

14. A model in macroeconomics is a logical, mathematical, and/or computational framework designed to describe the operation of a national or regional economy, and especially the dynamics of aggregate quantities such as the total amount of goods and services produced, total income earned, the level of employment of productive resources, and the level of prices.

There are different types of _____ that serve different purposes and have different advantages and disadvantages. Models are used to clarify and illustrate basic theoretical principles in macroeconomics; they are used to test, compare, and quantify different theories of the macroeconomy; they are used to produce 'what if' scenarios, and especially to evaluate the possible effects of changes in monetary, fiscal, or other macroeconomic policies; and they are used for generating economic forecasts.

   a. Factor shares
   b. High-powered money
   c. Natural rate of unemployment
   d. Macroeconomic models

15. A variety of measures of _____ and output are used in economics to estimate total economic activity in a country or region, including gross domestic product (GDP), gross national product (GNP), and net _____

There are three main ways of calculating these numbers; the output approach, the income approach and the expenditure approach. In theory, the three must yield the same, because total expenditures on goods and services must equal the total income paid to the producers (Gnational income), and that must also equal the total value of the output of goods and services (GNP.)

   a. GNI per capita
   b. Gross world product
   c. Volume index
   d. National Income

16. _____ use double-entry accounting to report the monetary value and sources of output produced in a country and the distribution of incomes that production generates. Data are available at the national and industry levels.

The NIPA summarizes national income on the left (debit, revenue) side and national product on the right (credit, expense) side of a two-column accounting report.

a. Net national product
b. Current account
c. Gross private domestic investment
d. National Income and Product Accounts

17. The Organisation for Economic Co-operation and Development (_____) is an international organisation of 30 countries that accept the principles of representative democracy and free-market economy. Most _____ members are high-income economies with a high HDI and are regarded as developed countries.

It originated in 1948 as the Organisation for European Economic Co-operation, led by Robert Marjolin of France, to help administer the Marshall Plan for the reconstruction of Europe after World War II.

a. AD-IA Model
b. ACEA agreement
c. ACCRA Cost of Living Index
d. OECD

18. In finance, a _____ is a debt security, in which the authorized issuer owes the holders a debt and, depending on the terms of the _____, is obliged to pay interest (the coupon) and/or to repay the principal at a later date, termed maturity. A _____ is a formal contract to repay borrowed money with interest at fixed intervals.

Thus a _____ is like a loan: the issuer is the borrower (debtor), the holder is the lender (creditor), and the coupon is the interest.

a. Zero-coupon
b. Prize Bond
c. Callable
d. Bond

19. The term _____ refers to government debt, expenditures and revenues, or to finance (particularly financial revenue) in general.

- _____ deficit is the budget deficit of federal or local government
- _____ policy is the discretionary spending of governments. Contrasts with monetary policy.
- _____ year and _____ quarter are reporting periods for firms and other agencies.

a. Bucket shop
b. Drawdown
c. Procter ' Gamble
d. Fiscal

20. In economics, _____ is the use of government spending and revenue collection to influence the economy.

_____ can be contrasted with the other main type of economic policy, monetary policy, which attempts to stabilize the economy by controlling interest rates and the supply of money. The two main instruments of _____ are government spending and taxation.

a. 100-year flood
b. Sustainable investment rule
c. Fiscal policy
d. Fiscalism

21. _____ and Keynesian Theory) is a macroeconomic theory based on the ideas of 20th-century British economist John Maynard Keynes. _____ argues that private sector decisions sometimes lead to inefficient macroeconomic outcomes and therefore advocates active policy responses by the public sector, including monetary policy actions by the central bank and fiscal policy actions by the government to stabilize output over the business cycle.

The theories forming the basis of _____ were first presented in The General Theory of Employment, Interest and Money, published in 1936.

a. Keynesian economics
b. Market failure
c. Rational choice theory
d. Deflation

22. _____ is the process by which the government, central bank (ii) availability of money, and (iii) cost of money or rate of interest, in order to attain a set of objectives oriented towards the growth and stability of the economy. Monetary theory provides insight into how to craft optimal _____.

_____ is referred to as either being an expansionary policy where an expansionary policy increases the total supply of money in the economy, and a contractionary policy decreases the total money supply.

a. 1921 recession
b. 130-30 fund
c. 100-year flood
d. Monetary policy

23. In economics, the _____ is a historical inverse relation between the rate of unemployment and the rate of inflation in an economy. Stated simply, the lower the unemployment in an economy, the higher the rate of increase in nominal wages in the economy. Rate of Change of Wages against Unemployment, United Kingdom 1913-1948 from Phillips (1958)

William Phillips, a New Zealand born economist, wrote a paper in 1958 titled The Relationship between Unemployment and the Rate of Change of Money Wages in the United Kingdom 1861-1957, which was published in the quarterly journal Economica.

a. Cost curve
b. Demand curve
c. Lorenz curve
d. Phillips curve

24. _____ refers to the objective and subjective components of the believability of a source or message.

Traditionally, _____ has two key components: trustworthiness and expertise, which both have objective and subjective components. Trustworthiness is a based more on subjective factors, but can include objective measurements such as established reliability.

a. 130-30 fund
b. Credibility
c. 100-year flood
d. 1921 recession

25. _____ is an assumption used in many contemporary macroeconomic models, and also in other areas of contemporary economics and game theory and in other applications of rational choice theory.

Chapter 27. Epilogue: The Story of Macroeconomics

Since most macroeconomic models today study decisions over many periods, the expectations of workers, consumers, and firms about future economic conditions are an essential part of the model. How to model these expectations has long been controversial, and it is well known that the macroeconomic predictions of the model may differ depending on the assumptions made about expectations

    a. Minimum wage   b. Potential output
    c. Balanced-growth equilibrium   d. Rational expectations

26. _____ is an economic situation in which inflation and economic stagnation occur simultaneously and remain unchecked for a period of time. The portmanteau _____ is generally attributed to British politician Iain Macleod, who coined the term in a speech to Parliament in 1965. The concept is notable partly because, in postwar macroeconomic theory, inflation and recession were regarded as mutually exclusive, and also because _____ has generally proven to be difficult and costly to eradicate once it gets started.
    a. Chronic inflation   b. Real interest rate
    c. Stagflation   d. Price/wage spiral

27. The _____ says that it is naïve to try to predict the effects of a change in economic policy entirely on the basis of relationships observed in historical data, especially highly aggregated historical data.

The basic idea pre-dates Lucas's contribution, but in a 1976 paper he drove home the point that this simple notion invalidated policy advice based on conclusions drawn from estimated system of equation models. Because the parameters of those models were not structural - that is, not policy-invariant - they would necessarily change whenever policy - the rules of the game - was changed.

    a. Dahrendorf hypothesis   b. Demand management
    c. Lucas critique   d. Peak-load pricing

28. _____ is a branch of applied mathematics that is used in the social sciences (most notably economics), biology, engineering, political science, international relations, computer science, and philosophy. _____ attempts to mathematically capture behavior in strategic situations, in which an individual's success in making choices depends on the choices of others. While initially developed to analyze competitions in which one individual does better at another's expense (zero sum games), it has been expanded to treat a wide class of interactions, which are classified according to several criteria.
    a. Discriminatory price auction   b. Game theory
    c. Proper equilibrium   d. Dollar auction

29. _____ in economics and business is the result of an exchange and from that trade we assign a numerical monetary value to a good, service or asset. If Alice trades Bob 4 apples for an orange, the _____ of an orange is 4 apples. Inversely, the _____ of an apple is 1/4 oranges.
    a. Premium pricing   b. Price war
    c. Price book   d. Price

30. _____ is a concept with somewhat disparate meanings in several fields. It also has a common meaning which has a loose connection with some of those more definite meanings.

Casually, it is typically used to denote a lack of order, or purpose, or cause.

a. 100-year flood
c. 1921 recession
b. Randomness
d. 130-30 fund

31. A _____, sometimes denoted _____, is a mathematical formalization of a trajectory that consists of taking successive random steps. The results of _____ analysis have been applied to computer science, physics, ecology, economics, and a number of other fields as a fundamental model for random processes in time. For example, the path traced by a molecule as it travels in a liquid or a gas, the search path of a foraging animal, the price of a fluctuating stock and the financial status of a gambler can all be modeled as _____s.

a. 1921 recession
c. 100-year flood
b. 130-30 fund
d. Random walk

32. The Dornbusch _____ or Exchange rate overshooting, first established by economist Rudi Dornbusch, aims to explain why exchange rates have a high variance. The key insight of the model is that lags in some parts of the economy can induce compensating volatility in others.

Dornbusch developed this model back when many economists held the view that ideal markets should reach equilibrium and stay there.

a. International investment position
c. International finance
b. Overshooting model
d. Optimum currency area

33. _____ is a school of contemporary macroeconomics that strives to provide microeconomic foundations for Keynesian economics. It developed partly as a response to criticisms of Keynesian macroeconomics by adherents of New Classical macroeconomics.

a. Mainstream economics
c. New Keynesian economics
b. Law of demand
d. Keynesian theory

34. _____ Theory (or _____ Theory) is a class of macroeconomic models in which business cycle fluctuations to a large extent can be accounted for by real (in contrast to nominal) shocks. (The four primary economic fluctuations are secular (trend), business cycle, seasonal, and random.) Unlike other leading theories of the business cycle, it sees recessions and periods of economic growth as the efficient response to exogenous changes in the real economic environment.

a. Real business cycle
c. SIMIC
b. Monetary policy reaction function
d. Balanced-growth equilibrium

35. _____ is a class of macroeconomic models in which business cycle fluctuations to a large extent can be accounted for by real (in contrast to nominal) shocks. (The four primary economic fluctuations are secular (trend), business cycle, seasonal, and random.) Unlike other leading theories of the business cycle, it sees recessions and periods of economic growth as the efficient response to exogenous changes in the real economic environment.

a. Real business cycle theory
c. Consumer spending
b. Solow residual
d. War economy

Chapter 27. Epilogue: The Story of Macroeconomics

36. In economics, _____ is the total supply of goods and services produced by a national economy during a specific time period. It is the total amount of goods and services in the economy available at all possible price levels.
    a. Aggregate supply
    b. Aggregation problem
    c. Aggregate expenditure
    d. Aggregate demand

37. _____ is widely regarded as the first modern school of economic thought. It is the idea that free markets can regulate themselves. Its major developers include Adam Smith, David Ricardo, Thomas Malthus and John Stuart Mill. Sometimes the definition of _____ is expanded to include William Petty, Johann Heinrich von Thünen.
    a. Schools of economic thought
    b. Tendency of the rate of profit to fall
    c. Classical economics
    d. Marginalism

38. _____s is the social science that studies the production, distribution, and consumption of goods and services. The term _____s comes from the Ancient Greek οἰκονομία from οἶκος (oikos, 'house') + νόμος (nomos, 'custom' or 'law'), hence 'rules of the house(hold)'. Current _____ models developed out of the broader field of political economy in the late 19th century, owing to a desire to use an empirical approach more akin to the physical sciences.
    a. Inflation
    b. Opportunity cost
    c. Energy economics
    d. Economic

39. _____ is an economic model based on price, utility and quantity in a market. It predicts that in a competitive market, price will function to equalize the quantity demanded by consumers, and the quantity supplied by producers, resulting in an economic equilibrium of price and quantity. The model incorporates other factors changing equilibrium as a shift of demand and/or supply.
    a. Deferred gratification
    b. Joint demand
    c. Rational addiction
    d. Supply and demand

40. In economics, endogenous growth theory or _____ was developed in the 1980s as a response to criticism of the neo-classical growth model.

    In neo-classical growth models, the long-run rate of growth is exogenously determined by either assuming a savings rate (the Harrod-Domar model) or a rate of technical progress (Solow model.) However, the savings rate and rate of technological progress remain unexplained.

    a. Kondratiev waves
    b. New growth theory
    c. Real prices and ideal prices
    d. Cobweb model

41. _____ is a branch of economics that deals with the performance, structure, and behavior of a national or regional economy as a whole. Along with microeconomics, _____ is one of the two most general fields in economics. It is the study of the behavior and decision-making of entire economies.
    a. New Trade Theory
    b. Macroeconomics
    c. Tobit model
    d. Nominal value

ANSWER KEY

Chapter 1
1. d	2. c	3. d	4. d	5. b	6. c	7. c	8. c	9. a	10. a
11. c	12. d	13. b	14. c	15. d	16. b	17. d	18. a	19. a	20. d
21. d	22. a	23. d	24. a	25. d					

Chapter 2
1. b	2. c	3. a	4. a	5. b	6. d	7. a	8. d	9. b	10. c
11. d	12. b	13. b	14. c	15. d	16. a	17. d	18. b	19. d	20. c
21. a	22. d	23. d	24. a	25. d	26. c	27. d	28. b	29. a	30. a
31. b	32. d	33. a	34. b	35. b	36. a	37. d	38. a	39. d	

Chapter 3
1. a	2. d	3. d	4. a	5. d	6. d	7. d	8. d	9. d	10. a
11. c	12. d	13. b	14. d	15. a	16. b	17. d	18. b	19. c	20. d
21. b	22. c	23. d	24. d	25. a	26. b	27. b	28. a	29. c	30. d
31. d	32. d	33. d	34. d	35. d	36. d				

Chapter 4
1. a	2. d	3. a	4. d	5. d	6. d	7. d	8. c	9. d	10. d
11. d	12. d	13. b	14. d	15. b	16. a	17. a	18. d	19. a	20. b
21. b	22. d	23. d	24. b	25. d	26. d	27. b	28. d	29. b	30. d
31. b	32. a	33. b	34. d	35. d	36. b				

Chapter 5
1. d	2. c	3. d	4. a	5. c	6. a	7. a	8. a	9. d	10. b
11. c	12. d	13. d	14. c	15. c	16. d	17. d	18. b	19. c	20. b
21. b									

Chapter 6
1. c	2. a	3. d	4. d	5. c	6. b	7. b	8. a	9. c	10. d
11. d	12. c	13. d	14. a	15. b	16. c	17. a	18. d	19. d	20. c
21. b	22. d								

Chapter 7
1. b	2. d	3. a	4. d	5. d	6. d	7. b	8. c	9. b	10. d
11. c	12. a	13. d	14. b	15. b	16. a	17. d	18. c	19. b	20. d
21. c	22. a								

Chapter 8
1. d	2. d	3. d	4. c	5. a	6. a	7. a	8. b	9. b	10. b
11. b	12. d								

Chapter 9
1. d	2. b	3. c	4. b	5. d	6. a	7. d	8. d	9. a	10. d
11. c	12. b	13. b	14. a	15. d					

Chapter 10
1. c   2. a   3. d   4. d   5. d   6. d   7. c   8. b   9. d   10. a
11. d   12. b

Chapter 11
1. d   2. c   3. d   4. a   5. c   6. a   7. c   8. d   9. b   10. d

Chapter 12
1. a   2. c   3. b   4. c   5. d   6. d   7. d   8. a   9. d   10. d
11. a   12. d   13. d   14. d   15. d   16. b   17. c   18. c   19. c   20. b
21. d

Chapter 13
1. d   2. d   3. b   4. d   5. a   6. a   7. d   8. b   9. b   10. d
11. d   12. c   13. a   14. a   15. d   16. d

Chapter 14
1. b   2. d   3. b   4. b   5. d   6. d   7. d   8. d   9. d   10. d
11. d   12. a   13. a   14. d   15. d   16. d

Chapter 15
1. a   2. d   3. b   4. d   5. b   6. c   7. b   8. b   9. b   10. d
11. d   12. d   13. a   14. c   15. d   16. a   17. c   18. a   19. d   20. d
21. d   22. a   23. a   24. d   25. d   26. b   27. c   28. a   29. d   30. a

Chapter 16
1. a   2. d   3. d   4. d   5. d   6. d   7. b   8. d   9. b   10. d
11. d   12. d   13. b   14. d   15. d   16. d   17. d   18. d   19. b

Chapter 17
1. a   2. b   3. b   4. b   5. a   6. d   7. d   8. d   9. b

Chapter 18
1. a   2. d   3. d   4. a   5. d   6. c   7. d   8. a   9. a   10. d
11. b   12. b   13. d   14. c   15. d   16. c   17. a   18. d   19. d   20. d
21. c   22. d   23. c   24. b   25. b   26. d   27. a   28. d

Chapter 19
1. d   2. b   3. a   4. b   5. d   6. d   7. b   8. d   9. a   10. d
11. d   12. c   13. c   14. d   15. d   16. d   17. d   18. d

ANSWER KEY

Chapter 20
1. b   2. b   3. d   4. a   5. d   6. d   7. c   8. c   9. d   10. a
11. d 12. c 13. d 14. b 15. d 16. d 17. d 18. d 19. d 20. a
21. d 22. b 23. d 24. d 25. d 26. b 27. b 28. b

Chapter 21
1. d   2. b   3. a   4. d   5. d   6. b   7. a   8. d   9. b   10. d
11. d 12. b 13. b 14. d 15. d 16. d 17. d 18. c 19. a 20. c
21. d 22. c 23. c 24. b 25. a 26. a

Chapter 22
1. a   2. d   3. d   4. a   5. d   6. d   7. d   8. c   9. a   10. d
11. b 12. d 13. a 14. b 15. a 16. b 17. d 18. d 19. a 20. d
21. b

Chapter 23
1. d   2. b   3. b   4. b   5. a   6. d   7. d   8. d   9. d   10. c
11. c 12. d 13. a 14. c 15. c 16. c 17. d 18. d 19. d 20. a
21. d 22. a 23. b

Chapter 24
1. d   2. b   3. c   4. d   5. d   6. d   7. a   8. d   9. b   10. c
11. c 12. d 13. d 14. b 15. c 16. b 17. b 18. d

Chapter 25
1. a   2. d   3. d   4. a   5. b   6. d   7. d   8. d   9. a   10. a
11. d 12. a 13. b 14. d 15. d 16. d 17. d 18. a 19. c 20. c
21. d 22. b 23. a 24. b 25. a 26. d 27. b 28. d 29. b 30. d
31. b

Chapter 26
1. d   2. c   3. d   4. d   5. b   6. b   7. d   8. d   9. c   10. a
11. a 12. d 13. d 14. b 15. d 16. c 17. d 18. a 19. d 20. a
21. d 22. d

Chapter 27
1. d   2. d   3. d   4. a   5. d   6. d   7. d   8. a   9. d   10. a
11. b 12. d 13. b 14. d 15. d 16. d 17. d 18. d 19. d 20. c
21. a 22. d 23. d 24. b 25. d 26. c 27. c 28. b 29. d 30. b
31. d 32. b 33. c 34. a 35. a 36. a 37. c 38. d 39. d 40. b
41. b

www.ingramcontent.com/pod-product-compliance
Lightning Source LLC
Chambersburg PA
CBHW082041230426
43670CB00016B/2737